Social Media Marketing

A Complete Guide For Social Media Marketing How To Grow Your Business And To Execute Sales

JOHN JOHNSON

© **Copyright 2020 by (John Johnson) - All rights reserved.**

This document is geared towards providing exact and reliable information in regards to the topic and issue covered. The publication is sold with the idea that the publisher is not required to render accounting, officially permitted, or otherwise, qualified services. If advice is necessary, legal or professional, a practiced individual in the profession should be ordered. From a Declaration of Principles which was accepted and approved equally by a Committee of the American Bar Association and a Committee of Publishers and Associations. In no way is it legal to reproduce, duplicate, or transmit any part of this document in either electronic means or in printed format. Recording of this publication is strictly prohibited and any storage of this document is not allowed unless with written permission from the publisher. All rights reserved.

The information provided herein is stated to be truthful and consistent, in that any liability, in terms of inattention or otherwise, by any usage or abuse of any policies, processes, or directions contained within is the solitary and utter responsibility of the recipient reader. Under no circumstances will any legal responsibility or blame be held against the publisher for any reparation, damages, or monetary loss due to the information herein, either directly or indirectly. Respective authors own all copyrights not held by the publisher. The information herein is offered for informational purposes solely, and is universal as so. The presentation of the information is without contract or any type of guarantee assurance. The trademarks that are used are without any consent, and the publication of the trademark is without permission or backing by the trademark owner. All trademarks and brands within this book are for clarifying purposes only and are the owned by the owners themselves, not affiliated with this document.

Contents

Introducing 4
Chapter 1 6
Social media Marketing 6
1.1 What is Marketing for Social Media? 6
1.2 Marketing of social media for small and local enterprises 12
1.3 What are marketing strategies? 19
1.4 What is Organic Social Media marketing ? 21
Chapter 2 27
In sport, social media marketing 27
   2.1 In sports, what part does social media marketing play? 27
   2.2 Intensify fans' passion? 28
   2.3 How to market sports using social media? 29
   2.4 Examples of social media use by sports teams and athletes 31
Chapter 3 32
Companies and Social Media 33
   3.1 How are businesses supported by social media? 32
   3.2 Ads for Businesses in Social Media? 34
   3.3 How to pick the right marketing social media platforms? 36
Chapter 4 43
Current and future of ads on social media 43
   4.1 At present, Social Media 43
   4.2 The near future of marketing on social media 45
   4.3 Future of social media marketing 67
Chapter 5 70
The Marketing Plan for Social Media 70
   5.1 Introducing 70
   5.2 Digitalization in Business" National Level Seminar 76
Conclusion 86

Introduction

In different respects, technical advances have a tremendous effect on any organization. The advent of internet technology has revolutionized marketing practices worldwide (Baird & Parasnis, 2011). There is strong consumer competition today, and consumers have the ability to make smarter choices on the selection of products and services available. The organizations ought to be cautious in this dynamic situation to maintain the allegiance of the customer

. Reducing the trust distance between the enterprise and the client may be a positive way to build a stronger connection that will also help establish a better understanding of the customer's needs and desires. In this respect, social media plays a vital role, and businesses profit from the friendly approach to social media to create brand relationships ships (Hachinski et al., 2010).

The contact links used to link persons together are social networking platforms. Data has shown that consumers turn towards using social media to obtain access to information, ideas, and resources (Donath, 2004). Social media technologies have changed the strategies for handling the interaction between brands and consumers. Social media's strength lies in the fact that it has created how individuals engage with each other. They were able to retain ties with each other (Pauwels, 2004).

To foster the brands, advertisers use social media platforms. They use social media to consider consumer desires and then build effective techniques to enable their offerings to accomplish the marketing target (Donath, 2004). To initiate dialogues, connectivity is critical and valuable. However, communication is the only mechanism used to initiate, grow, and sustain the interaction between two entities. Communication opens opportunities for conflict and the eradication of misunderstanding (McEwen, 2005). Social networking acts as a forum for the collaboration and interaction of a diverse range of clients.

Companies will increase awareness of their brands through this medium. Through disseminating their specialty and point of parity, they may also market their products (Breivik & Thorb-jørnsen, 2008). Social media platforms have made engagement and collaboration too convenient for various businesses to communicate with their consumers and recognize their interests, which are then used offline to establish effective brand marketing strategies (Brakus et al., 2009). While contact and face-to-face conversation are solid, social media offers an important communication substitute. It helps to handle the exchange of instant messaging and dialogues between brands and clients. These sites can store the conversation between the brands and consumers and can be used for further development. Brands can also flash their ads on social networking sites. It's like winning a bid to flash the advertisements on the intended audience's sites. In presenting their advertisements, brands have to realize that they have to win the deal. They must state their target group specifically and put the highest bids. This results in the development of visibility for multiple consumers, which can indirectly lead to large revenue and a massive fan base for a company.

Social media sites are not only a trend to be pursued. Rather they have shown their value in establishing a brand's relationship with the consumer, capturing new buyers, maintaining customers, high-end advertising scheme, and potential development of the brand. Companies should not continue to neglect such a critical medium for the growth of their brand. Conrad et al. (2010) said that the most current marketing contact is social media and social networking platforms.

The web provides a more transparent and unrestricted means of contact for advertisers. The new website age has more inclusive services for consumers, and advertisers use these facilities. The protection of modern websites is growing, which also improves consumer trust in the organization's online purchasing of goods. Yahoo, Twitter, and LinkedIn, and other similar social networking platforms, draw millions of people.

In these social networking sites, advertisers search for their clients and use them as marketing channels and contact with customers. Simultaneously, as checking and sharing information, clients collect information from social networking networks here. The consistency and authenticity of such data are more than how consumers trust each other.

Chapter 1: Social media Marketing

1.1 What is Marketing for Social Media?

To advertise a product or service, social media marketing uses social media channels and websites. While e-marketing and digital marketing are still prevalent in academia, social media marketing is becoming more common for practitioners and researchers.

Most social media sites have built-in analytical tools for data, allowing businesses to monitor ad campaign progress, effectiveness, and engagement. Via social media marketing, companies target various stakeholders, including current and potential clients, current and potential staff, journalists, writers, and the general public.

Social media marketing at a strategic level involves managing a marketing strategy, governance, setting the scope for the more active or passive use), and establishing the ideal social media "culture" and "tone." of an organization.

Companies may encourage consumers and Internet users to post user-generated content (e.g., online feedback, product reviews, etc.), often known as "earned media," utilizing social media ads rather than marketer-prepared promotional copy.

Websites for Social Networking

Websites for social networking allow individuals, companies, and other organizations to connect and create online relationships and communities. Consumers can communicate with them directly when businesses enter these social channels.

The interaction can be more personal to consumers than conventional outbound marketing and advertisement methods. Social networking sites serve as word of mouth or, more specifically, e-word of mouth. The Internet's capacity to reach billions across the globe gave a strong voice and far reached to online word of mouth.

An influence network is described as the ability to rapidly alter purchasing habits and the purchase and operation of goods or services for a growing number of consumers. Social networking sites and blogs enable followers to "retweet" or "repost" comments made by others about a product being promoted, which occurs very frequently on certain social media sites. By repeating the message, the link of the user is linked. Since the product information is put out there and replicated, more traffic is brought to the product/company

Websites for social networking are focused on developing virtual communities that allow customers to communicate their wishes, desires, and values online. Marketing on social media then links these customers and viewers to companies who have the same desires, wishes, and values. Companies may keep in contact with individual followers through social networking sites. This personal contact will instill in followers and potential customers a feeling of loyalty.

Products may also hit a tiny target audience by selecting who to follow on these platforms. Social networking sites also give us a lot of knowledge about which potential consumers may be involved in products and services. Marketers can identify purchase signs, such as content exchanged by individuals and questions posed online, using emerging semantic analysis technologies. An awareness of purchasing signs will help salespeople target specific prospects, and marketers manage micro-targeted campaigns.

Over 80% of business executives described social media as an important part of their organization in 2014. Business retailers have seen a 133% rise in their social media marketing revenues.

Facebook, Instagram, Twitter, TikTok, MySpace, and Snapchat are some examples of popular social networking websites over the years.

Mobile handsets

In the world, over three billion people are involved on the Internet. The Internet has increasingly gained more and more users over the years, jumping [9] Approximately 81 percent of the United States' existing population has social media profiles that they regularly connect with. Due to their web surfing capabilities, cell phone use is useful for social media marketing. By allowing customers to access pricing and product details in real-time quickly, cell phones have altered the path-to-purchase process.

They have also helped businesses to regularly alert and update their followers. Many businesses now placed QR (Quick Response) codes and items to access their smartphones on the company website or online services. By linking the code to brand websites, ads, product information, and any other mobile-enabled content, retailers use QR codes to promote customer engagement with brands. Also, real-time bidding in the mobile advertising industry is high and growing due to its value for web browsing on-the-go. Nexage, a real-time bidding provider for mobile ads, announced a 37 percent rise in revenue per month in 2012. Another mobile advertising publication site, Adfonic, announced a rise of 22 billion ad requests in the same year.

Mobile devices have become increasingly popular, with 5.7 billion people worldwide using them. Media communicate with viewers and has many more ramifications for TV ratings, ads, mobile commerce, and more. The consumption of mobile media, such as mobile audio streaming or mobile video, is increasing.

More than 100 million users are expected to access online video content via mobile devices in the United States. Mobile video revenue is made up of downloads, advertisements, and subscriptions for pay-per-view. As of 2013, internet user penetration of cell phones worldwide was 73.4 percent. In 2017, statistics showed that more than 90 percent of Internet users use their phones to access online content. As a marketing tool, there are two specific techniques for using social media:

Passive methodology

Social networking can be a valuable source of consumer data and a way for customer viewpoints to be understood. Blogs, content groups, and forums are sites where people post their reviews of brands, products and services, and suggestions.

Businesses can tap and analyze customer voices and feedback generated for marketing purposes in social media; For example, videos and photos of the iPhone 6 "bend test" The dispute over the so-called "bend gate" created frustration among customers who had waited months to launch the new iPhone rendition. However, Apple immediately released a statement stating that the problem was exceptionally unusual and that the company took several steps to make a case for the mobile device.

Sturdier and heavier. Unlike conventional market research approaches such as time-consuming and expensive surveys, focus groups, and data mining, which take weeks or even months to study, marketers may use social media to collect "live" or "real-time information on customer behavior and points of view on the brand or goods of a business. In the highly complex, competitive, fast-paced, and global marketplace of the 2010s, this could be useful.

Active Approach

Social media can be used as public relations and direct marketing tools and as communication platforms that target particular audiences as effective customer interaction tools with social media influencers and social media personalities. This strategy is commonly known as influencer marketing. Influencer marketing offers advertisers the ability to reach their target audience through a special community of chosen influencers promoting their product or service in a more honest, authentic way.

In reality, according to Business Insider Intelligence estimates, brands are expected to spend up to 15 billion on influencer marketing by 2022, based on Mediakix data.

Technologies that predate social media, such as broadcast TV and newspapers, may also provide a reasonably targeted audience for advertising since an advertisement inserted during a sports game broadcast or in a newspaper's sports section is likely to be read by sports fans. Social networking networks can, however, much more effectively target niche audiences. Advertisers can target their ads to particular audiences using digital tools such as Google Adsense, such as individuals involved in social entrepreneurship, political advocacy affiliated with specific online posts, and social media users' comments. It will be difficult for a TV station or paper-based newspaper to have targeted advertisements.

In certain cases, social networks are regarded as a perfect tool for preventing expensive market analysis. They are renowned for offering a short, easy, and direct way to reach an audience through a well-recognized individual. For instance, an athlete supported by a sporting goods company often brings millions of people interested in what they do or how they perform to their support base.

Now they want to be part of this athlete by endorsing that specific company. Consumers would visit shops at one point to see their goods with popular athletes, but now. He specifically advertises them to you via his accounts on Twitter, Instagram, and Facebook.

Facebook and LinkedIn are leading sites for social media where users can hyper-target their advertising. Hyper targeting uses information from the public profile and submits information to users but hides it from others.

There are many examples of businesses introducing online dialogue with the public to improve customer relations. "Business executives such as Jonathan Swartz, President, and CEO of Sun Microsystems, Apple Computers CEO Steve Jobs, and Bob Langert, Vice President of McDonald's, regularly post in their CEO blogs, encouraging customers to communicate and freely express their feelings, ideas, suggestions, or comments about their posts, the company or its product.

Social Media participation ensures that clients and customers are active participants rather than passive viewers. Consumer advocacy groups and groups that criticize businesses are examples of this (e.g., lobby groups or advocacy organizations). Social media enables all consumers/citizens to express and share an opinion about an organization's goods, services, business practices, or actions in a commercial or political sense. When other customers read their positive or negative comments or feedback, each participating customer, non-customer, or citizen participating online through social media becomes part of the marketing department (or a challenge to the marketing effort).

It is necessary for effective social media marketing to get users, potential customers, or people to be engaged online. With the introduction of social media marketing, it has become increasingly important to gain customer interest in goods and services. In a political sense, this can finally be converted into purchasing actions or voting and donating behavior. New engagement and loyalty models for online marketing have emerged to create customer participation and brand credibility.

Social media interaction for a social media campaign is divided into two parts. The first is the constructive, frequent uploading of new material online. This can be seen by images, digital videos, email, and conversations that are digital. It is also expressed through the sharing of other people's content and information through web links. The second aspect is reactive conversations with social media users who respond by posting or messaging to those who reach your social media profiles. Conventional media such as TV news shows are restricted to one-way customer contact or 'push and tell.' Only particular information is presented to the customer with little or minimal customer feedback mechanisms.

Traditional newspapers, such as physical journals, offer readers the right to write a letter to the editor. However, since the editorial board needs to review the letter and determine if it is suitable for publication, this is a relatively slow process. On the other hand, social networking is participative and open; users can instantly express their opinions on brands, goods, and services. The conventional media gave the message's marketer control, while social media transfers the equilibrium to the consumer or citizen.

1.2 Marketing of social media for small and local enterprises

As a promotional technique, small companies also use social networking sites. Companies may follow social networking sites by individuals in the local area to advertise specials and promotions. They can be exclusive and get a free drink with a copy of this tweet" in the form. This message encourages other locals to follow the company on the platforms to receive the promotional deal. The organization gets seen and promotes itself in the process (brand visibility).

Businesses can gain useful insights into whether or not a product can be embraced by their target market enough to warrant full production by allowing their clients to provide input on new product concepts. Besides, consumers will believe that the company has engaged them in the co-creation process. The company uses customer input to develop or change a product or service that fills the target market with a need. Such input can come in various ways, such as surveys, competitions, polls, etc.

Social networking sites such as LinkedIn often allow small companies to find applicants to fill staff roles.

Review sites such as Yelp, of course, also assist small companies in developing their credibility beyond just brand visibility. Strong consumer peer reviews help to affect potential prospects rather than market ads to buy products and services.

Nike launched its social media initiative, Make It Count, in early 2012. The campaign launch began with the launch of a YouTube video by YouTubers Casey Neistat and

Max Joseph, where they traveled 34,000 miles to visit 16 cities in 13 countries. They promoted the hashtag #makeitcount, which millions of customers shared via Twitter and Instagram by uploading images and sending tweets. The YouTube video #MakeItCount went viral, and in 2012, the year this product was launched, Nike saw an 18 percent rise in profit.

As a networking tool that makes businesses available to those interested in their product and makes them visible to those who do not know their products, one of the key goals of using social media in marketing. These companies use social media generate buzz and learn from. Target consumers form of marketing that can attract customers at any point in the consumer decision-making journey. There are also other benefits of marketing via social media. Seven of the top 10 variables that correlate with a successful organic search by Google rely on social media.

Google searches appear less. While platforms like Twitter, Facebook, and Google have a greater number of monthly users, mobile platforms focused on visual media sharing, however, obtain a higher rate of engagement compared to them and have reported the fastest growth and changed how customers e With an average of 130 million monthly users, Instagram has an interaction rate of 1.46 percent compared to Twitter, which has an interaction rate of .03 percent with an average of 210 million monthly users.[29] Unlike conventional media, which are also cost-prohibitive for many businesses, a social media strategy does not entail astronomical budgeting.

To this end, businesses use channels such as Facebook, Twitter, YouTube, and Instagram to reach markets far wider than using conventional print/TV/radio advertising alone at a fraction of the Customers can now post product and service reviews, rate customer service, and directly answer questions or voice complaints to businesses via social media channels. According to Measuring Performance, more than 80 percent of customers use the web to research goods and services. To create relationships of confidence with customers, social media marketing is often used by businesses.

To this end, companies may often employ workers to specifically manage these social networking interactions, which are typically listed under the title of Online Community Managers. Handling these relationships satisfactorily will lead to an improvement in consumer confidence. 3 steps are taken to resolve customer issues, define the extent of social chatter, engage influencers to assist, and create a proportional response to both this objective and repair the public's view of a brand.

Twitter enables businesses to advertise their goods in short messages known as tweets limited to 140 characters that appear on followers' Home timelines. Tweets can include text, hashtag, photo, video, animated GIF, emoji, links to the product's website and other social media profiles, etc.[35] Companies are now using Twitter to provide customer service.[36] Several businesses support

There are many more comprehensive Facebook pages than Twitter accounts. They make it possible for a product to have videos, images, longer descriptions, and testimonials that followers can comment for anyone to see on the product pages. As well as sending out event updates, Facebook will connect back to the product's Twitter page. As of May 2015, 93 percent of marketers in companies use Facebook to promote their brand. 84 percent of "engagement" or clicks and likes connected to Facebook ads were attributed to a 2011 study.[38]

By 2014, Facebook had reduced the content published from company and brand pages. Facebook algorithm changes had decreased the audience for non-paying business pages (with at least 500,000 "Likes") from 16% in 2012 to 2% in February 2014.

With LinkedIn

A professional business-related networking platform, LinkedIn enables companies to build professional profiles to network and meet others for themselves and their business. Members can promote their social networking activities, such as Twitter streams or blog posts, through widgets.[43] LinkedIn offers its members. Also, businesses have shown a preference for the amount of data that can be accessed from a LinkedIn profile versus a restricted email

WhatsApp

Jan Koum and Brian Acton formed X. WhatsApp continues to run as a separate app, joining Facebook in 2014, with a laser emphasis on creating a messaging application that works easily and efficiently anywhere in the world. WhatsApp also facilitates the sending and receiving a range of media, including text, images, videos, documents, locations, and voice calls, as an alternative to SMS. WhatsApp messages and calls are encrypted with end-to-end encryption, ensuring they can not be read or listened to by any third party, including WhatsApp. In over 180 countries, WhatsApp has a consumer base of 1 billion people. [47] [48] It is used to give individual customers personalized promotional messages. It has several advantages over SMS, including controlling how Message Broadcast works in WhatsApp using the blue tick option. It allows messages to be sent to customers of Do Not Disturb (DND).

WhatsApp is often used to deliver a series of bulk messages using broadcast options to their targeted customers. Companies have begun to use this largely because it is a cost-effective advertising option and a message transmitted rapidly. WhatsApp also does not authorize companies to put advertisements in their applications as of 2019.

Yelp Yelp

Yelp consists of a detailed database of company profiles online. Similar to Yellow Pages, businesses are searchable by the venue. In seven separate nations, including the United States and Canada, the website is operational. Holders of a business account are permitted to build, post, and edit business profiles. They can post information about the company's location, contact information, photographs, and information about the service. The website also enables users to compose, post company reviews, and rate them on a five-point scale. For general users of the website, messaging and talk functions are also made available to direct ideas and opinions.

Inside Instagram

Instagram had over 200 million users in May 2014. Instagram's user engagement rate was 15 times higher than Facebook's and 25 times higher than Twitter's. According to Scott Galloway, L2's founder and a marketing professor at the Stern School of Business at New York University, recent studies report that 93 percent of prestigious

This smartphone app is now being used extensively by several brands to improve their marketing campaign. Instagram can be used to gain the requisite traction to catch the consumer segment's attention interested in the supply of goods or services. Because Apple and Android sponsor Instagram, users of smartphones can easily access it.

Also, it can be accessed through the Internet as well. Therefore, marketers see it as a potential forum for expanding their public visibility, especially to the younger target group. Also, advertisers use social media for conventional internet ads and inspire consumers to pay attention to a specific brand. In general, this provides an incentive for greater exposure to the brand.

Advertisers also use the platform to push social shopping and encourage individuals to collect and post pictures of their favorite items. Starbucks, MTV, Nike, Marc Jacobs, and man more like Red Bull are big examples of multinationals that adopted the mobile photo app early on. Many names have already jumped on board.

Fashion blogger Danielle Bernstein, who goes on Instagram through @weworewhat, partnered with Harper's Bazaar to do a piece on how companies use Instagram to sell their goods and how it makes money for bloggers. Instagram followers and whose "outfit of the day" pictures on Snapchat receive tens of thousands of screenshots, clarified that she must feature the brand in a certain number of posts for many of her sponsored posts, and sometimes can not wear the product of a competitor in the same image. According to Harper's Bazaar, industry figures suggest that brands spend more than $1 billion a year on consumer-generated ads.

Instagram founder Kevin Systrom also went to Paris Fashion Week to go to couture shows and meet designers to learn more about how style bloggers, writers, and designers actually control most of his application content.

Instagram has proved itself a strong forum for advertisers to post pictures and short messages to meet their consumers and prospects. 71 percent of the biggest brands in the world are now using Instagram as a marketing platform, according to a survey by Simply Measured. Instagram can be used as a medium for businesses to link and interact with current and future consumers.

The company can portray a more intimate image of their brand, and by doing so, the company conveys a stronger and more real image of itself. On-the-go is the definition of Instagram photos, a sense that the event is occurring right now, and that adds another dimension to the company's personal and accurate photo. In reality, Thomas Rankin, co-founder and CEO of Dash Hudson claimed that his only negative feedback is if it looks too posed when he approves a blogger's Instagram post before it is posted on behalf of a brand his company supports. It's not an editorial photo, "It's not an editorial photo, "We're not trying to be a magazine. We're trying to create a moment."We're not trying to be a magazine. We're trying to create a moment."

On Snapchat

Snapchat is a popular application for messaging and image sharing developed by three Stanford University students in 2011. The application was first created to allow users to send back and forth messages and images that are only usable for 1-10 seconds until they are no longer available. The app was an immediate success among social media members, and up to 158 million people use Snapchat every day today. It is also estimated that Snapchat users open the app approximately 18 times a day, meaning that users are on the app for about 25-30 minutes a day.[61]

YouTube Programs

Another famous medium is YouTube; ads are done to suit the target audience in a way. The kind of vocabulary used in the advertisements and the thoughts used to advertise the product represents the viewer's style and taste. The advertisements on this site are usually aligned with the requested video content; another benefit that YouTube brings to advertisers. Some advertisements, because the content is appropriate, are provided with such images. On YouTube, advertising opportunities such as funding a video are also possible, such as a user searching for a YouTube.

"A video on dog training can be presented in results along with other videos with a sponsored video from a dog toy company." YouTube also allows publishers to earn money through its YouTube Partner Program. Companies will pay YouTube for a special "channel" promoting products or services for companies.

Pages for social bookmarking

Each of these sites is dedicated to collecting, curating, and organizing links to other websites that users consider to be of good quality. This process is crowdsourced, allowing members of amateur social media networks to sort and prioritize links by r

Blogs Over

Platforms such as LinkedIn provide an online connection environment for businesses and customers. Businesses that understand the need for content, originality/and accessibility use blogs to make their goods famous and unique/and eventually reach customers who are privy to social media.2009 studies show that customers view media or blogger coverage as being more.

The "Largest in-stream ad unit on the web" sponsored web post that attracts users' attention when viewing their Dashboard via their computer or laptop. It also allows viewers to like, reblog, and share it.

Based on their originality and creativity, Radar picks up outstanding posts from the entire Tumblr community. It is placed next to the Dashboard on the right side, and it usually receives 125 million daily impressions.

Sponsored Spotlight-Spotlight is a directory of some of the community's popular blogs and places where new blogs can be found for users to follow. Advertisers can choose one category from fifty categories to list their blog to differentiate the promoted posts from regular user posts. Tumblr announced customization and themes on mobile apps for brands to advertise on May 6, 2014.

1.3 What are marketing strategies?

To successfully advertise online, social media marketing includes the use of social networks, consumer online brand-related activities, and electronic word of mouth.

Social networks such as Facebook, Tinder, and Twitter provide advertisers with information about their customers' likes and dislikes. This technique is crucial because it provides companies with a "target audience" A good service will result in a positive rating via social media that gets the hotel free ads. However, a bad service will result in a negative customer review that could theoretically damage the company's credibility.

The buzz of word of mouth marketing has all been influenced by social networking sites such as Facebook, Instagram, Twitter, MySpace, etc. Misner said in 1999 that word-of-mouth marketing is the world's most effective, yet least understood marketing strategy" (Trusov, Bucklin, & Pauwels, 2009, p. 3). [80]. Through the power of opinion leaders, the rise in the use of social media and smartphones is attributed to the increased online "buzz" of "word-of-mouth" marketing encountered by a product, service or organization.

Businesses and advertisers have found that many small groups influence personal behavior" (Kotler, Burton, Deans, Brown, & Armstrong, 2013, p. 189). Such small groups circulate social networking accounts that are run by prominent individuals with group followers (opinion leaders or "thought leaders"). The categories of groups (followers) are referred to as: reference groups (people who meet each other either face-to-face or have an indirect impact on the attitude or behavior of an individual); affiliation groups (a person has a direct influence on the attitude or behavior of a person); and ambition groups (groups which an individual wish to belong to).

Marketers target prominent individuals on social media, known as influencers, who are identified as opinion leaders and opinion-formers to deliver messages to their target audiences and amplify their effect. A social media app by an opinion leader may have a much greater effect than a social media posts by a daily user (via the forwarding of the post or the' like' of the post).

Marketers recognize that "consumers are more prone to believe in other individuals" (Sepp, Liljander, & Gummerus, 2011). OLs and OFs can also send messages of their own about the products and services they choose (Fill, Hughes, & De Francesco, 2013, p. 216). The reason for the strong following basis for the leader or opinion formators is that their opinion is valued or trusted (Clement, Proppe, & Rott, 2007).

For their follow-up, they will check goods and services, which can be positive or negative towards the company. OL's and OF's are individuals with social standing and can affect other individuals because of their appearance, views, values, etc. (Kotler, Burton, Deans, Brown, & Armstrong, 2013, p. 189).

They typically have many followers known as their party of reference, membership, or aspiration (Kotler, Burton, Deans, Brown, & Armstrong), 2013, p. 189. The following may be impacted by getting an OL or OF endorse a brand and because they trust the OL/OF to have a high chance of the brand selling more goods or building a following base. Getting an OL/OF helps spread word of mouth between reference groups and/or membership groups, such as families and colleagues.

The modified contact model illustrates the usage of opinion leaders and opinion leaders. The sender/source provides the message to many, many OL's/OF's who, along with their personal opinion, pass on the message, form their own opinion of the recipient (followers/groups), and give their personal message to their community (friends, relatives, etc.) (Dahlen, Lange, & Smith, 2010, p. 39).[86]

1.4 What is Organic Social Media marketing?

Owned social media networks are an integral extension of the world of today's business and brands. On each platform, the brand must build its brand image and appeal to the type of customer audience on each respective platform.

In comparison to pre-Internet marketing, such as TV advertising and newspaper advertisements, in which the marketer managed all aspects of the ad, users are free to post feedback about their product right below an online advertisement or an online post by a company. As part of their conventional marketing campaigns using magazines, newspapers, radio ads, television advertisements, companies are gradually using their social media strategy. Since media users have often used several channels simultaneously in the 2010s (for example, browsing the Internet on a tablet while watching a live TV show), marketing content needs to be consistent across all platforms, whether conventional or new media.

Heath (2006) wrote about the scope of exposure that corporations can provide to their websites on social media. It is a question of seeking a balance between posting regularly but not over posting. As people need notifications to gain brand awareness, there is a lot of attention paid to social media platforms. A lot more content is therefore required, and this can sometimes be unplanned content.

The designed content starts with the creative/marketing team creating their concepts, and they send them off for approval after they have finished their ideas. There are two general approaches to doing so. The first is where each market, editor, brand, followed by the legal team, approves the proposal one after another (Brito, 2013). Depending on the size and physical of the company, sectors will vary.

The second is where 24 hours (or other allocated time) are given to each sector to sign off or disapprove. The original plan is executed if no action is taken during the 24-hour span. Planned content is always obvious to consumers and is un-original or lacks excitement, but it is also a better choice to prevent unwanted public backlash. As in the above, all paths for planned content are time-consuming; it takes 72 hours to approve the first way of approval. Although the second path can be significantly shorter, especially in the legal department, it also carries more risk.

Unplanned material is an idea of a spontaneous, tactical reaction" (Cramer, 2014, p. 6). The material could be trendy and not have the time to take the route of the expected content. The unplanned content is released sporadically and is not organized by calendar/date/time (Deshpande, 2014). Concerns with unplanned content revolve around legal problems and whether the message sent reflects the company/brand appropriately. If a business sends a Tweet or Facebook message too fast, it can inadvertently use insensitive language or messaging to alienate some customers.

For example, after she made a social media post commenting about HIV-AIDS and South Africa, celebrity chef Paula Deen was criticized; her message was considered offensive by many observers. The key difference between scheduled and unplanned is the period for the material to be accepted. Unplanned content, for example, 1-2 hours or less, must still be accepted by marketing managers, but in a much faster way.

Sectors can miss errors because of being rushed. "If they occur, be prepared to be reactive and adapt to challenges." Crisis escalation plan, "Crisis escalation plan, "It will happen" It will happen. The solution includes separating the issue into subjects and classifying the problem into groups. The color-coding of the potential danger of "identifying and flagging potential risks" also helps to coordinate a problem. The dilemma can then be handled and dattempting to solve the situation.

Implications for traditional advertising

The minimization of consumption

Print and television ads use conventional advertising strategies. As the largest advertisement market, the Internet has already overtaken television. Banner or pop-up advertisements are also included on web pages. Pages for social networking don't always have commercials. Items, in turn, have whole pages and can communicate with users.

Television commercials often finish with a spokesman telling viewers to look out for more information on the product page. Print advertising, though briefly common, had QR codes on it. Cell phones and computers will search these QR codes, sending viewers to the product's website. Advertising is starting to shift audiences from conventional to electronic outlets. While traditional media and TV advertising are increasingly overshadowed by social media marketing, traditional marketing still has a position. For newspapers, for instance, readership has seen a decline over the years. Nevertheless, journal readership is also intensely loyal to print-only newspapers. 51% of newspaper subscribers only read the newspaper in its print form, making it useful for well-placed advertising.

Leaks Over

One of the challenges facing conventional ads is the Internet and social networking leaks. Video and print commercials are frequently leaked across the Internet to the world sooner than they are expected to debut. Social networking platforms cause these leaks to go viral and be viewed more easily by many users. The disparity in time is also a concern confronting conventional advertisers.

There is sometimes a delay between airings on the eastern coast and the west coast of the United States when social issues arise and are shown on television. Social networking sites have become a center of event-related comments and conversation. This makes it possible for people watching the event (time-delayed) on the west coast to know the result before it airs. The 2011 Grammy Awards illustrated this dilemma. On the west coast, audiences discovered who received various awards based on comments made by people watching live on the east coast on social networking sites. [94] Because viewers knew who won already, many tuned out, and ratings were lower. As audiences had no incentive to watch, all the publicity and promotion put into the event was lost. [According to whom?

The Mishaps

Marketing on social media offers a way for companies to communicate with their clients. Organizations must, however, safeguard their data and closely track feedback and complaints on the social media they use. A flash survey conducted on 1225 IT executives from 33 countries found that social media mishaps caused a combined $4.3 million in losses to organizations in 2010.

The top three social media accidents experienced by a company during the previous year included workers revealing too much information in public forums, losing or exposing sensitive information, and growing litigation exposure.

Gap sent a tweet to its followers in 2012 during Hurricane Sandy asking them to stay healthy but urged them to shop online and give free shipping. The tweet was considered disrespectful, and Gap finally took it down and apologized. There are several additional instances of online marketing mishaps. Examples tell a YouTube video of a Domino's Pizza Hutt person breaching health code guidelines that went viral on the Internet and later culminated in criminal charges against two employees. A Twitter hashtag was posted by McDonald's in 2012, gaining publicity due to various grievances and adverse incidents encountered by customers in the chain store, and a Chrysler Community posted a 2011 tweet.

In 2018, after opposing government measures to improve conditions for domestic workers.

Ethics in

Social media can also be linked to the code of ethics associated with conventional marketing. But with social media being so personal and foreign, there is another list of complexities and difficulties that come with being ethical online. Social media marketing practices' objective is a sensitive topic for social media practitioners, specifically: the proper use of, often very personal data. The marketer no longer has to rely exclusively on the simple demographics and psychographics generated by television and magazines with the advent of social media. Still, now they can see what people want to hear from advertisements. Nevertheless, social networking sites are becoming aware of these activities and are effectively weeding out and banning criminals.

Furthermore, social media sites have become increasingly conscious of their users and gather information about their viewers in different ways to communicate with them. The Facebook Inc. social networking platform is quietly working on a new advertising framework that will allow advertisers to target users with advertisements based on the vast quantities of information that people share about themselves on the site. This could be an immoral or ethical aspect for some people.

Some individuals may respond negatively because they think it is a privacy invasion. On the other hand, since their social network knows their interests and sends them unique ads relating to those interests, some people can appreciate this function. Consumers want to network with individuals that share their values and desires.

Individuals who agree to create a public social media profile should be aware of the willingness of advertisers to take information that interests them and be able to send them content and advertising to improve their sales. To build relationships and connect with clients, managers engage in social media.

Strategists and advertisers have been smarter and more cautious about gathering information and delivering ads since social media marketing came into being. This can be seen as a wide field that is ethically grey. This is a privacy infringement for many people, but there are no regulations that stop these businesses from utilizing the information given on their websites. Companies such as Equifax, Inc., TransUnion Corp, and LexisNexis Group are active in gathering and distributing social media users' personal information. In 2012, Facebook purchased information from a third-party firm named Datalogix from 70 million households. Facebook later announced that the data was purchased to create a more successful advertisement service.

In 2016, Facebook had an estimated 144.27 million views, about 12.9 million each month. Despite this high amount of traffic, the millions of users who log in to Facebook and other social media sites each month have done very little to protect them. President Barack Obama sought to negotiate with the Federal Trade Commission (FTC) to control data mining. He introduced the Privacy Bill of Rights, which would protect the average user from accessing and exchanging private information with third-party businesses. The proposed legislation would allow the customer greater power over what information corporations would collect. President Obama was unable to pass any of these laws through Congress, and concerning social media marketing ethics, it is unclear what President Trump will do.

Chapter 2: In sport, social media marketing

2.1 In sports, what part does social media marketing play?

Social media marketing in sport has increased, as sports teams and clubs understand the importance of social media relationships with their fans and other audiences. Sports figures such as Cristiano Ronaldo have 40.7 million Twitter followers and 49.6 million Instagram followers, creating opportunities for endorsements

Any sports franchise aims to have a committed, involved fan base. Thus, embracing social networking networks such as Facebook, Twitter, and Instagram to deepen and expand their relationships with fans has become an absolute no-brainer for professional sports teams. There are some significant ways in which social media helps it to happen.

Developing new team storytelling tools

Social media is essentially a storytelling tool, and it's here that it has been so influential in helping the wider public sell sports franchises themselves. This is possible to use social media to tell an underdog's tale, share success stories when a team is doing well, and increase rivalries with some teams. Simultaneously, TV has always been good at displaying some natural rivalries, such as Yankees vs.

Establish one-on-one ties with star athletes

In the sports marketing industry, what has changed most is building apparent relationships with marquee athletes who have their own personal social media accounts. For their favorite stars, fans will definitely tune in to a Facebook Live stream or find their favorite players' share on Instagram.

Every major athlete has their own Twitter account these days, and there is an incredible amount of giving and taking between these professional athletes and their followers.

"Particularly if in fantasy sports leagues, these fans happen to own" them). It is now also the case that social media players may become fan favorites and help form the narratives that appear in the mass media.

2.2 Intensify fans' passion?

There will be a groundswell of excitement and pride every time an underdog team becomes a challenger or if a team pulls off a major upset. In the past, all that enthusiasm and pride may have been difficult to channel, but now it is possible to intensify fans' passion on a game-by-game basis. As new hashtags become popular, they can be easily spread through all social media channels, such as the New Orleans Saints' #whodathashtag. Trends that once took weeks to create and evolve now seem to occur overnight.

Build real-time, immersive experiences involving fans

It is now possible to use them to construct new types of interactive interactions, considering the real-time existence of social media sites such as Twitter. The Boston Red Sox, for example, would communicate with their fans via Twitter during rain delays, asking them to send suggestions for music to play while waiting for their team to re-take the field. Some professional sports teams use Twitter to perform blitz surveys. All is in the interest of having a better experience for fans.

Overall, there has been a huge influence of social media on sports marketing. The industry continues to develop and grow, continually discovering new ways to expand and deepen connections with fans by using social media. Every sports team's dream is to capture an invested fan base's excitement and attention, and social media makes it much easier on a year-round basis to do so.

2.3 How to market sports using social media?

349Sports Marketing and Social Media Sports Marketing in several contexts, the word 'marketing' is used. Some think of marketing as using ads, advertising, and personal selling tactics to make a product recognizable to others or encourage more buyers to buy it. Market-ing, however, is much more detailed than this narrow conception.

Simply put, marketing involves focusing on fulfilling the needs and wishes of consumers or clients. In essence, this means that sports marketing focuses on satisfying the needs of sports customers or customers, including people who engage in playing sports, viewing or listening to sports news and programmers, collecting memorabilia, purchasing apparel, buying sports products such as jerseys and shoes, or even browsing a sports website to find out the latest on their favorite team, player or sports website. A consumer of sport is anyone who normally uses goods or services for sport. A sports client is someone who pays for a particular product or service to be used (BLlythe, 2005).

It is acceptable to refer to those people who use and pay for sports products and services to use the terms interchangeably. Sport Is a Unique ProductSports marketing is the combination of marketing concepts for sports services and products and marketing through sports events of non-related sports products (Merz, 2008). Therefore, sports marketing has two primary dimensions.

First, the use of general marketing practices for sporting goods and services is significant. The second is the promotion, by sport, of other industrial goods or services. Sport marketing tracks, like any other marketing, to satisfy customers' needs and desires. It does this by supplying customers with sport-related goods and services. However, sports marketing is distinct from formal marketing because it also has the capacity to facilitate the consumption of non-sport goods and services by associations.

It is rational to understand that sports marketing means sports marketing and sport as a tool to market other products and services. For example, sporting equipment, professional competitions, sports events, and local clubs could include marketing sports products and services directly to sports customers. Selling season tickets, team ads, planning a promotional stunt to promote an athlete, and creating licensed merchandise for sale are other examples. Marketing by sport occurs when a sports organization sells a non-sport object.

Some examples could include a well-known athlete endorsing a biscuit, a company sponsoring a sports event, or even beverage companies arranging to have exclusive rights to provide drink at a sports venue or event (Coca Cola n.d.). The two aspects of sports marketing are essential to understanding the full range of ways in which sport is used. However, the weakness is that sports marketing's sale aspect appears to focus (Smith A., 2008).

To figure out what sports clients want and the best ways to achieve it are a long-term strategic review must be prepared before any dealing occurs. Consequently, sports marketing should also be regarded as a set of planning and performance activities related to delivering a sports product or service. A sports product or service must take place in the mind of a consumer before any sales. In reality, a consumer is aware of these needs and has reacted to the sports product or service somehow. The process of creating such a reaction is known as branding, and when a sports brand has found a firm place in the minds of consumers, it can be said that it is positioned (Smith A Z., 2008a).

The result of successful branding and strong market position is a single transaction, and establishing a steady relationship between a sports brand and sports marketing.

Facebook and Twitter are the most prominent social media networks, but athletes and teams still use marketing sites, including Instagram and Snapchat. As for other industries, the benefits of using social media in sports include building brand recognition, quickly and cost-effectively reaching a wider audience, developing brand supporters, and engaging loyal sports fans. For advertisements and promotions, there are several examples of athletes and sports teams using social media.

2.4 Examples of social media use by sports teams and athletes

Michigan Presale Incentive: To find greater exposure, Michigan used a very clever way to maximize the total number of likes" or "followers" for its Facebook and Twitter accounts. Fans are expected to follow" or like" their Facebook or Twitter page at the largest football arena in the nation 'The Big House' to have the ability to apply for pre-sale tickets for their Michigan football games. This helps them to be able to buy pre-sale tickets for any game they want, making this marketing tactic a perfect tool for their team and many other items to raise awareness.

Louisville Slugger Scavenger Hunt: Hillerich & Bradsby, manufacturers of Louisville Slugger bats and other baseball equipment, developed a scavenger hunt via Twitter to raise awareness of their business after the St. Louis Cardinals won the World Series in 2011. The search included 45 commemorative bats from the World Series dispersed around the city of St. Louis, Missouri. The Twitter page of the Louisville Slugger posted "tweets" indicating where the bats were located within the area. To keep up to date on the particular "tweets" relating to the hunt, the fan or participants used their cell phones.

This company conducted a scavenger hunt to find attention and increase their number of Twitter followers. The figures show that their fan base skyrocketed, increasing by 143 percent the number of Facebook likes by 834 percent the number of people talking about the brand on Facebook, and 161 percent the number of Twitter followers.

Several athletes, including Kobe Bryant, Russell Wilson, and Rafael Nadal, have used social media to promote their fans and enhance their brand awareness. Athletes have also promoted brands via social media, including the sponsorship of Recovery Water by Russell Wilson and Wheels Up's promotion by Serena Williams. These fan-based website pages have increased dramatically in numbers because of this marketing tool, giving them the exposure they were looking for.

Bringing all of this together

Since the 1870s, sports and famous athletes have been an omnipresent part of marketing in this country and remain one of the most important instruments for reaching consumers. They will set themselves up for greater success as teams and brands find new ways of harnessing and incorporating fan excitement into their customer service efforts.

Teams can understand real consumer engagement outcomes by supporting the athletes as the public wants to see them, using those athletes in experiential marketing, and engaging fans via social media.

Chapter 3: Companies and Social Media

3.1 How are businesses supported by social media?

Today, social media and social networking platforms are the best way for a company to communicate with potential customers since they enable businesses to reach potential customers without investing exorbitant amounts of advertising money.

Social networking allows continued brand presence and brand interaction through engaging interactions that can often be of little to no financial cost to businesses, promoting brand recognition and loyalty. By engaging with them at a more meaningful level, these digital media encourage viewers' public trust. For many brands, social media marketing is the latest motto; social networking traders take notice of many possibilities for social media and begin to accomplish new social improvisation at a higher pace than ever before.

Marketing of social media and the companies that take advantage of it have become more experienced (Almotairi, 2014). Not surprisingly, companies of all kinds and sizes use social media for marketing and fuss in public relations. The growth of social media and sequential developments in technology obviously generate incomparable and exceptional prospects for those willing to invest in them.

And for enterprises, it offers a marketing opportunity that overcomes and explicitly links the conventional medium with consumers. Many companies are exploring social media marketing campaigns, from giants like Starbucks and IBM to small ice cream shops (Neti, 2011). Marketers were unsure about the use of social media for the business not so long ago. But in 2013 (more than 3000 marketers, according to a survey in the USA), a significant 86 percent of marketers said that social media is important to their businesses (Stelzner, 2013). In the early days, emails, and websites first supported businesses; the next wave of marketing is social media. Marketing today has a radically different scope and return, with social media's appearance (Story, 2007).

Social networking provides a two-way connection between the entity and the user, where both can communicate with each other. Mangold and Faulds (2009) noticed nine ways in which businesses use social media effectively. It can be one of the practical examples for a win-win situation; the customer can state his opinion and get a response, while the business gets to dive deep into customer care and distinguish their overall performance.

Wright, Khanfar, Harrington, and Kizer (2010) hypothesize that it is becoming more successful than conventional marketing, communication, and advertisement approaches to use mobile technology to reach consumers... In targeting new audiences and tailoring the message based on each customer, social media efforts, especially mobile technology, are becoming more valuable.

3.2 Ads for Businesses in Social Media?

Marketing on social media is a powerful way to reach prospects and clients for organizations of all sizes. Your customers are already engaging through social media with brands, and you're missing out if you're not talking directly to your audience with the help of social networks such as Facebook, Twitter, Instagram, and Pinterest! Social media marketing will bring your company success, building loyal brand advocates, and even driving leads and sales.

To be your marketing and branding objectives, social media marketing, or SMM, is a type of internet marketing that involves making and sharing content on social media networks. Social media marketing involves sharing notifications of text and photos, videos, and other material that drives user interaction and ads on paid social media.

We've built this guide to give you an introduction to social media marketing and some tips and training for starting social media marketing to enhance your company's social presence.

You can begin designing your own expert strategy for social media marketing with these tips.

Marketing and Social Media: Begin with a Plan

Consider the priorities of your organization before you start designing social media marketing campaigns. Without a social strategy in mind, starting a social media marketing campaign is like wandering around a forest without a map. You might have fun, but you're probably going to get lost.

When determining your social media marketing targets, here are some questions to ask:

What do you intend to accomplish through the marketing of social media?

- **Who is the target audience?**

Where would your target audience be hanging out, and how would social media be used? With social media marketing, what message do you want to send to your audience?

Your type of company should educate and drive your marketing plan for social media.

For instance, being highly visual, an e-commerce or travel company can get a lot of value from a strong Instagram or Pinterest presence. On Twitter or LinkedIn, a business-to-business or marketing company may find more leverage.

How Marketing for Social Media will help you achieve your marketing objectives

Marketing on social media can help with a variety of objectives, such as:

Increasing traffic from websites Check out our best marketing tips for social media

EVER! Free Download Here.

Best Tips for Ads on Social Media

Social Media Content Planning-As previously mentioned, it is important to develop a social media marketing strategy.

Great social content: content reigns supreme when it comes to social media marketing, consistent with other online marketing fields.

A Clear Brand Image helps your company to project your brand image across several different social media channels by using social media for marketing. Although each platform has its own unique atmosphere and voice, your company's core personality should remain changed.

Curating and linking to outside sources insane trust and reliability, and in exchange, you can also get some connections.

It is always important to keep watching competitors that can provide useful information for keyword analysis and other social media marketing insights.

Measuring the success of social media through Twitter Analytics

Measuring success with analytics-Without monitoring data, you can not assess your social media marketing strategies' success... Add monitoring tags to your marketing campaigns on social media so that you can manage them properly. And be sure to use the analytics for even more insight into which of your social content performs best with your audience within each social network.

Social Media Crisis Management: With brands on social media, things don't always go swimmingly.

3.3 How to pick the right marketing social media platforms?

Here's if we sum up using social media according to the specific user base and marketing climate. Different marketing websites for social media need different approaches, creating a specific approach customized for and platform.

Using Facebook for Marketing Social Media

For Social Media Ads using Google+

As a Facebook rival, Google+ joined the scene, but it now serves a more niche audience. It won't work for everybody, but on Google+, some communities are really involved.

You can upload and share images, videos, links, and view all your +1s on Google+. Use Google+ circles to divide your followers into smaller groups, allowing you to share data with some followers while barring others. You might try to build a "super-fan" circle, for example, and only share exclusive deals and exclusive offers with that party.

Remember that Google has confirmed plans to delete Google+, so prepare accordingly!

Using Pinterest for Marketing Social Media

One of the fastest-growing apps in social media marketing is Pinterest. Pinterest's image-centered platform is suitable for retail, but for social media purposes or sales-driving advertising, everyone can profit from using Pinterest.

Using Twitter for Marketing Social Media

Twitter is a social networking advertisement site that will help you transmit your messages over the internet. Join tweeters in your business or similar places, and you will receive a constant stream of followers in response.

With fun, brand-building tweets about specials, deals, and headlines, mix the official tweets. When a customer has something positive to tell for you, make sure to retweet, and when appropriate, don't hesitate to answer user queries. Using Twitter as a social networking marketing tool revolves around conversation and touch, so make sure to communicate as much as possible to nurture and improve your fans.

Using LinkedIn for Social Network Ads

LinkedIn is one of the most proficient social network marketing sites. LinkedIn Communities are a great opportunity for individuals in different fields to join in professional dialogue and offer a forum for like-minded people to exchange knowledge. It is also suitable for workers for a job posting and general networking. The advantage of ranking on Google's video search results is also added to these how-to tutorials, so don't underestimate video material's power!

Social Networking Resources Focused on Location

Platforms.YouTube is the number one site for creating and distributing video material and can also be an incredibly successful social network marketing platform. Many businesses want to produce video content to make their video go viral." Still, in practice, those chances are very slim. Instead, focus on creating interesting, informative videos of how-to" for social media such as Yelp and FourSquare are great for brick and mortar companies trying to incorporate social media marketing.

Register on these sites to assert your location position, and consider extra perks, including check-in incentives or exclusive discounts.

You know, these visitors are going to hold their phones in their possession, encourage customers or clients to send the company a recommendation on your LinkedIn profile. Recommendations help the firm look more reliable and trustworthy to prospective buyers. Browse LinkedIn's Questions section as well; having responses enables you to become a thinking leader and build trust.

Social Media Ads

To write reviews and upload them. Many good reviews will greatly help to influence future visitors to come in and develop your company!

Use Reddit for Marketing Social Media

Reddit, or related social networking platforms like Stumble Upon or Digg are great for posting persuasive information.

Reddit has excellent

social networking sites, social media marketing Potential of more than 2 billion page views each month, but marketers should be warned that it would only allow truly initial, interesting content. Posting on Reddit is playing with fuel, posting spam or blatantly sales-focused material, and this incredibly tech-savvy community might berate the organization.

If you have material that you feel the Reddit audience would enjoy (most are young, geeky, liberal, and fascinated with the internet), you might reap tremendous benefits and receive valuable traffic.

Using social media in ads does more than increasing web traffic and helps companies attract more customers; it offers a powerful platform for the target audience to understand better and learn.

Paying Tips for Social Media Marketing

We love paid social advertising because in an extremely cost-effective way, it expands the reach. If you play your cards right, you can have your material and offers in front of a huge audience at a meager expense.

Many social media platforms offer extremely granular targeting capabilities, enabling you to concentrate your budget on precisely the types of individuals most likely to be interested in your business. Some tips and tools for getting started with paid social media marketing are given below:

Small Company Social Media Ads

Social media on four main networks: Facebook, Twitter, LinkedIn, and Google+.

Build Successful Advertising on Facebook Most Social Media Keywords Checked - Common social media keywords.

Our 13 Best Tips Ever for Social Media Marketing –

The best of the best!

Do Advertising Work on Facebook? - Learn how and why Facebook ads operate.

5 Facebook Reasons to Advertise - If you're not even using Facebook ads, you can. And here's why!

Facebook Remarketing's Ridiculously Amazing Guide - For advanced Facebook advertisers. Learn how to recapture and close those leads for lost viewers!

Keyword Research for Social Media Experts Guide - Learn how to perform winning keyword research for different social media marketing strategies.

Social networking sites have a potential for social media marketing with more than 2 billion page views per month, but advertisers should be warned to accept only genuinely original, interesting content. Posting on Reddit is playing with fire, posting spam, or openly sales-focused content, and this extremely tech-savvy group could berate your company.

If you have content that you believe the Reddit community will appreciate (most are young, geeky, liberal, and obsessed with the internet), you could reap enormous benefits and gain valuable traffic.

The use of social media in ads increases web traffic and helps businesses attract more customers; it provides the target audience with a powerful platform to better understand and learn.

Social Media Marketing Paying Tips

We love paid social advertising because, in an extremely cost-effective way, it expands the reach. If you play your cards right, you can have your material and offers in front of a huge audience at a meager expense.

Many social media platforms offer highly granular targeting capabilities, allowing you to focus your budget on the kinds of people most likely to be interested in your company. Any tips and resources are offered below for getting started with paid social media marketing:

Small Social Media Ads Business

Four main networks have social media: Facebook, Twitter, LinkedIn, and Google+.

Building successful Facebook ads

Facebook may be one of the most efficient advertising outlets for moving your business forward. And that's not just to increase the brand's awareness. In this guide, you'll learn how to create powerful Facebook ads that generate real leads.

If you are already advertising on Facebook and looking to save time AND resources, check out WordStream Social Ads, our new product that allows Facebook advertising easier and more profitable.

How to build Twitter Advertising?

Ever businesses are not yet sure how to handle Twitter ads from a paid point of view. It's obviously not a one-size-fits-all endeavor, and you might wind up wasting a tonne of cash if you don't know precisely what you're doing. Learn how to master Twitter advertisements in this guide.

Chapter 4: Current and future of ads on social media

4.1 At present, Social Media

There are two main dimensions of the modern social media world. First, the main and small, existing, and emerging networks include the underlying technologies and business models that make up the industry and ecosystem. Secondly, the use cases are used, i.e., how these systems are used by different types of individuals and organizations and for what purposes.

Social media's growth has largely been influenced by its sites and how it has affected customer behavior and marketing practice. Some readers may remember social media's Bearly Days when social networking sites like MySpace and Friendster were popular. These websites have been precursors to Facebook and anything else that has changed in the last decade. We continue to have other types of social media alongside these channels, such as messaging (which began with simple Internet Relay Chat services in the 1990s and SMS text messaging built into early digital mobile phone standards in the 2000s) and asynchronous online conversations organized around particular topics of interest, for example, threaded discussion forums, subreddits on Reddit). We have recently seen the emergence of social media sites where text, including Instagram and Snapchat, is replaced by photos and videos.

The domestic business model has included monetization of users (audiences) across channels, traditionally and today, by providing advertising services to anyone seeking to target those audiences through digital content and marketing communications. Social media (in its different forms) for marketing purposes has been explored through prior study. Work by Leo et al. (2009) and Stephen and Galak (2012) showed for analysis that some forms of social interactions that are now happening on social media (e.g., Brefer a friend features and discussions in online communities) could have a positive effect on important marketing results such as acquisition and sales of new customers. More recently, the importance of social media ads continues to be discussed in media forms such as television (e.g., Fossen and Schweidel 2016, 2019) and impacts the acceptance of new goods through disseminating knowledge mechanisms (e.g., Hennig-Thurau et al. 2015).

While the rise and fall) of different types of social media sites has been important for understanding the social climate; we argue that understanding the current social media situation, at least from a marketing point of view, lies more in what users do on these platforms than in the technology or services provided by these platforms. People worldwide are actually using social media in different ways (e.g., Facebook and Twitter news feed, WhatsApp and WeChat private messaging, and Reddit discussion forums) for several purposes. This can typically be classified as:

Interacting and socializing digitally with known others such as family and friends. Doing the same but with known others but sharing common interests. Accessing and contributing to digital content such as news, gossip, and product reviews created by users.

Both of these instances of usage are simply WOM in one way or another. This, at least, as discussed by Lumberton and Stephen, is how marketing researchers have primarily characterized social media (2016). Indeed, online WOM has been and will continue to be relevant in marketing (e.g., the authors found, on average, a positive correlation between online WOM and sales in the meta-analysis by Babić Rosario et al. 2016).

The current social networking viewpoint is that people use it to build, access, and disseminate knowledge through WOM to various others, whether known as Bstrong ties^ or Break ties^ in their networks or unknown Bstrangers.^ Some recent research has looked at social media from the WOM perspective on the effects of WOM's dissemination (e.g., creating a Facebook post or tweeting) (e.g., Grewal et al. 2019; Hennig-Thurau et al. 2004; Hollenbeck and Kaikati 2012; Toubia and Stephen 2013; Wallace et al. 2014).

While this current WOM characterization appears to be true, social media is only considered from a communication viewpoint (and as a type of media channel). However, wider social ramifications are emerging as social media matures. We need to extend our outlook beyond the limited communicative aspects of so-called media to understand the future better and instead consider how customers will use it. Therefore, in the following parts of our vision for the future of social media in the industry, we aim to provide a more expansive view of social media (and will be) and explain why this view is important to market analysis and practice.

Overview of the system for the social media future in ads

In the following pages, when considering different related stakeholders, we present a structure for the immediate, near, and far future of social media marketing. Themes reflect those that already exist in the existing marketplace shortly, and those we expect will continue to form the social media landscape.

The near future segment discusses patterns that have shown early signs of manifesting and that we expect in the imminent future could dramatically shift the social media landscape. Finally, themes described as being in the far future are more theoretical predictions that we consider capable of shaping social media's future in the long term. The following parts dig through each of the themes in Table 1, grouped around the planned imminence of these themes' significance for marketing (i.e., the im- mediate, near, and far futures).

4.2 The near future of marketing on social media

In this segment, we highlight three trends that have arisen in the current environment to begin our debate on social media's direction, which we expect will continue to form the social media landscape shortly. The ever-changing digital and social media world we currently face is illustrated by these themes: Omni-social presence, the proliferation of influencers, and confidence and privacy issues. We assume that various stakeholders, such as individual social media users, businesses, and brands using social media, and public policymakers, will be impacted by these various fields (e.g., governments, regulators).

Presence on-social

Social networking practices were largely limited to designated social media sites such as Facebook and Twitter in their early days (or their now-defunct precursors). However, a proliferation of websites and apps that mainly serve seven-rate purposes has taken advantage of the ability to integrate social media features into their interfaces. Likewise, all major smartphone and desktop operating systems (e.g., sharing functions built into Apple's iOS) have in-built social media integration. This has made social media widespread and ubiquitous and has expanded the ecosystem beyond dedicated channels and maybe even omnipotent.

Consumers, thus, live in a world in which social media intersects with most facets of their lives through digital social interactivity in areas such Around the same time, conventional social media firms have extended their channels to offer a wider variety of features and services (e.g., the marketplace for Facebook, Chowdry 2018; payment system for WeChat, Cheng 2017). These bidirectional patterns indicate that in an increasingly Bomni-social environment, the modern-day customer lives.

The Bomni-social^ existence of the current world from a marketing point of view indicates that virtually every aspect of a customer's decision-making process is vulnerable to social media impact. When consumers watch their favorite beauty influencer trying a new product on YouTube, awareness of need can be triggered. Facebook friends what models they suggest, a consumer shopping for a car could search for details. To determine various lunch choices, a hungry employee could sift through Yelp reviews. To book future accommodation, a traveler could use Airbnb. Finally, an airline passenger who is highly dissatisfied (or delighted) could rant (rave) about their experience on Twitter. Although the decision-making funnel is arguably becoming flattered than the examples described above would indicate (Cortizo—Burgess 2014), these separate scenarios demonstrate that from start to finish, social media has the potential to affect the entire process of customer decision-making.

Finally, possibly the biggest sign of a Bomni-social^ phenomenon is how society itself continues to be influenced by social media. YouTube influencers, with their own TV shows (Comm 2016) and product lines, are now cultural icons (McClure 2015). Creative material on TV.

Films are also purposely meant to be Bgifable^ and meme-friendly (Bereznak 2018). Museums made-for-Instagram^ encourage creative content and experiences tailored for selfie-taking and sharing. These suggest that social media's influence is hardly limited to the world of Bonline (we address later in this paper the potential obsolescence of this term), but rather is constantly shaping cultural objects (television, film, the arts) that exceed its conventional limits. We assume that this pattern will continue to manifest, perhaps making the term Social media ^ out-of-date itself as the default expectation for customers, companies, and artists in different fields will be its omnipresence.

This Omni-social pattern raises several issues to be explored in future studies. For instance, in fields that have historically been non-social, how can social interactivity influence consumer behavior? It may also be insightful to discuss from a practitioner's perspective how advertisers can strategically approach the flatter decision-making funnel created by social media and to investigate how service providers can better alter experiential consumption while predicting the actions of social media sharing.

A well-known marketing technique is the concept of using celebrities (in consumer markets) or well-known opinion leaders (in business markets) who have high social value to influence others (Knoll and Matthes 2017). The omnipresence of social media, however, has significantly enhanced the accessibility and attractiveness of this strategy. For instance, Selena Gomez has over 144 million followers on Instagram who are engaged with each of her posts. The exposure of a single photo she shared was estimated at $3.4 million in 2018 (Maxim 2018).

She comes at a high price, though: one post that Selena supports for a brand will cost up to $800000000 (Mejia 2018). However, it may be somewhat speculative to place high valuations on mere online exposures or to collect Blikes^ for particular messages, as academic research shows that ac-quiring Blikes^ on social media can have little impact on the attitudes or behaviors of consumers (John et al. 2017; Mochon et al. 2017). Besides, Hennig-Thurau et al. (2015) suggest that although receiving positive WOM has little to no impact on consumer preferences; negative WOM may hurt customer preferences.

Although celebrities such as Selena Gomez are potential influencers for major brands, these typical celebrities are so costly that smaller brands have started and will continue to capitalize on the popularity and success of what is known as Bmicro-influencers, representing a new category of influencers. Micro-influencers are influencers who are not as popular as celebrities but who are influential and strong.

Enthusiastic follow-ups, typically more targeted, ranging from a few thousand to hundreds of thousands of followers (Main 2017). These influencers are usually considered more trustworthy and credible than conventional celebrities, which is a significant reason why influencer marketing has become increasingly attractive (Enberg 2018). In what they post about, these people are also seen as trustworthy experts, inspiring others to access the content they make and engage with them.

These influencers' use helps the brand reach customers more efficiently through first-person storytelling (compared to ads), which is considered warmer and more intimate and has been proven to be more effective in engaging consumers (Chang et al., 2019).

Considering the potential reach and involvement of social media influencers, businesses have either started to embrace social media influencers or plan to broaden their efforts in this area even further. For instance, in recent conversions we had with social media executives, some stated the increasing value of influencers. They mentioned how brands typically aim to integrate influencer marketing into their marketing strategies. Recent interviews with executives at some of the world's leading brands show that major brands' influencer marketing spending continues to grow.

Although social media influencer marketing is not new, we believe it has many potentials to grow further as an industry attempt. Duani et al. (2018) demonstrate that customers appreciate watching a live event even more and for longer periods of time than watching a pre-recorded one in a recent working paper. Therefore, we assume that live streaming by influencers will continue to expand, both in large and niche domains. Streaming video games on Twitch, a website owned by Amazon, for instance, may still be a niche, but it shows no signs of slowing down. Live channels, however, are constrained by the fact that the influencers need to sleep and do other offline tasks, being human. On the other hand, virtual influencers (i.e., BCGI^ influencers who look human but are not) have no such restrictions.

They're never sick or tired; they don't even eat unless expecting that virtual influencers will become even more popular on social media in the coming years, along with stronger computing power and artificial intelligence algorithms, being able to reflect and function on brand values invariably and interact with followers at any time.

There are several fascinating potential research avenues to be explored when thinking about social media influencers' position. First, marketers must decide what characteristics and qualities (e.g., authenticity, confidence, reputation, and liability) make supported posts by a conventional Understanding of what accomplishment has to do with real success.

Influencers' attributes, the type of content being shared, whether or not content is funded, and so on are important issues for businesses and social media sites when determinating relationships and where influencers can spend effort. Besides, research will help understand the appeal of live influencer content and how influencer content can be effectively combined with more conventional marketing mix strategies.

Concerns over social media privacy

There are no new customer questions about data protection and their capacity to trust brands and platforms (for a review on data privacy, see Martin and Murphy 2017). Marketing research and related fields have analyzed privacy and confidence concerns from various perspectives and have used different privacy concepts. Research has centered, for example, on the ties between personalization and privacy (e.g., Aguirre et al. 2015; White et al. 2008), the privacy relationship as it relates to customer trust and business efficiency (e.g., Martin 2018; Martin et al. 2017), and the legal and ethical implications. The way consumers, brands, policymakers, and social media networks evolve and adapt to these issues is still in flux and without definite resolution, despite this subject not sounding novel.

Making our interpretation of privacy issues even less simple is that a consistent definition of privacy is difficult to come by in current literature. In one privacy commentary, Stewart (2017) described privacy as being left alone, allowing a person to decide privacy invasions. We draw on this privacy concept to address a big privacy and trust issue late in the day

Specifically, how consumers adapt and respond to the modern world, where it is not possible to be left alone^ many con-summers would rather not share data and privacy for a more personalized experience, are dissatisfied with monitoring their purchases, and feel it should be illegal for brands to be able to purchase their data (Edelman 2018). These recent results seem to clash with previously developed work on standards of consumer privacy. Therefore, it is necessary to work in the future to understand if customers still respect in an ever-changing digital environment.

The way customers view brands and social media is becoming increasingly negative, in line with growing privacy concerns. Consumers remove their presence in social media, where research has shown that almost 40 percent of digitally linked people agree that at least one social media presence has been removed.

Media account owing to concerns about the mishandling of their sensitive details (Edelman 2018). For social media outlets and the marketers and marketers that have become reliant on these avenues to reach customers, this is a troubling development. Edelman noticed that about half of the customers surveyed felt that companies were involved in detrimental social network material facets, such as hate harassment, inappropriate content, or false news (Edelman 2018). Given that social networking has been one of the strongest ways for marketers to connect with users, create partnerships, and offer consumer support in terms of monitoring material, it is not only in the interest of social media sites for Bdo better, but the duty has been put on brands to advocate anonymity, trust, and the elimination of false or hateful information.

Therefore, in order to counteract these divisive market attitudes, anyone who profits from user interaction on social media would need to make improvements. Three big problems that erode customer interest need to be taken into consideration by social media sites and brands: personal knowledge, intellectual property, and information protection (Information Technology Faculty 2018).

Considering both of these issues, for better accountability and resulting confidence, concrete steps and measures need to be taken. We agree that marketers and agencies ought to keep social media responsible for their customer data activities, e.g., GDPR in the European Union) so that customers feel control of Bsafe ^ and Bin, ^ two considerations that have been found to be necessary in cases of privacy issues (e.g., Tucker 2014; Xu et al. 2012). Brands will develop consistent user data strategies in a manner that respects regulations, advertisement restrictions, and the right of a customer to privacy (a view shared by others; e.g., Martin et al. 2017). For brands to create feelings of faith in the extremely murky social networking domain, all of this is managerially important.

Future studies can assess customer responses to multiple forms of data and privacy updates and policies. Also, assessing the spillover impact of mistrust on social networking would be another related and significant path for potential studies. More precisely, if the site itself is distrusted, is all information posted on social media perceived as less trustworthy? Will this apply to web presentations of brand messages? Is there a negative spillover impact on other content posted across these channels created by users?

The Close Future

We addressed three places in the previous segment, where we think social networking is suddenly in flux. We discuss three patterns in this segment that have shown early signs of manifesting and that we expect will dramatically shift the social network environment in the immediate or not-too-distant future.

When addressing the immediate social network environment, these subjects affect the stakeholders we described.

Combating solitude and loneliness

In order to meet others, social networking has made things simpler. Bo's goal was to offer citizens the power to create communities and put the world closer together when Facebook was established in 2004. To keep connected with friends and family, to check out what's going on in the world, and to share and communicate what's important to them through Facebook (Facebook 2019).

Loneliness and loneliness remain on the rise amid this mission and the fact that consumers are more linked to other individuals than ever before. In the US, depression and alienation rates have doubled during the past fifty years, with Generation Z deemed the loneliest generation (Cigna 2018). Given these outcomes with the growth of social networking, the concern is that Facebook is messing with actual friendships and ironically spreading the loneliness it was supposed to conquer something to be considered (March 2012)?

The role of social media in loneliness is being heatedly debated. Any study has found that customer is adversely influenced by social media. Specifically, elevated social alienation, loneliness, and distress have been linked with heavy social media use. Furthermore, the usage of Facebook is adversely associated with customer wellbeing (Shakya and Christakis 2017), and correlational evidence has found that reducing the use of social networking to 10 minutes will alleviate feelings of alienation and distress due to fewer FOMO (e.g., Bear of losing out; ^ Hunt et al. 2018).

The usage of social media alone is not an indicator of depression since other variables must be weighed (Cigna 2018; Kim et al. 2009). In reality, although some research has shown that social networking has little impact on wellbeing, other research has shown that social media may support citizens across many various avenues, such as educating and improving socialization skills, facilitating greater connectivity and access to a greater wealth of resources, and helping to interact and belong (American Psychological Association 2011; Baker and Algorta 2016; Marker et al. 2018).

further suggests that most of the proof of user wellbeing usage of social media is of uncertain nature (e.g., limited and non-representative surveys, dependence on self-reported use of social media) and demonstrates that over time certain forms of use of social media are positively related to psychological wellbeing.

Managerially speaking, as a result of research highlighting a detrimental association between social networking and negative wellbeing, corporations are starting to re-spend. For e.g., Bedtime limit^ resources have been developed by Facebook (mobile operating systems, such as iOS, now also have these time-

Function Limiting). In specific users can also monitor their regular times, set up warning reminders that come up when the updates are reached by a self-imposed amount of time, and there is the ability to silence notifications for a set time span (Priday 2018). These numerous aspects appear well-intentioned and intended to offer a more favorable experience on social networking to individuals. It is unclear when these functions would be included.

Future studies will discuss whether or not users can utilize Btiming^ software accessible on one of the devices on which their social network resides (i.e., false self-policing) or simply to curtail the activity on any of their devices. It will also be the case that people invest less time on Facebook and Instagram but might spend the extra time on other rival social networking sites or hooked to smartphones, which would not help battle isolation potentially. A theoretically useful avenue for future study is learning how and which) customers utilize these self-control mechanisms and how impactful they are.

The standard of usage is one factor of social networking that has yet to be considered in the discourse on isolation by scientific tests (versus quantity). Facebook advertisements have started to suggest that Facebook isn't the strongest aspect of Facebook. This is why it makes us come together (Facebook, 2019). The authenticity of this type of messaging has been debated, but at its heart, in addition to encouraging disparities in quantity, it speaks to how users utilize the network.

Social networking sites can find new ways to build friend recommendations for people who have common interests and mutual friends to encourage in-person friendships to enhance this post (e.g., locational data from the mobile app service). There are applications that allow users to check for physically near buddies (e.g., Bumble Friends), and maybe social networking can go in the same path to counter the epidemic of isolation and remain present.

Future studies may investigate whether perceived isolation is causally influenced by the volume of usage, styles of social networking sites, or the manner social media is used. In particular, recognizing the detrimental associations observed between the usage of social media and wellbeing are related to the demographics of people accessing a lot of social media, the way social media functions or the way users want to communicate with the site would be crucial to consider the function (or lack of role of social media in the epidemic of isolation.

Customer service incorporated

As we know, customer service from digital platforms can shift drastically soon. To date, several companies have utilized social networking sites as a way to deliver consumer service, answer particular concerns from users, and resolve issues. Customer service focused on social networking is projected to become much more customized, personalized, and omnipresent in the future. Customers would be willing to communicate with businesses.

Anywhere and at any moment, answers to the issues of consumers would be more open and instant, or also preemptive using statistical techniques.

And today, we observe the gains that organizations gain from engaging with consumers on social media for service- or care-related purposes

Customer support is implemented in dedicated mobile applications and by direct messages on social media sites. Nevertheless, corporations tend to try to make things far easy for clients to engage with them anytime and wherever they may need it. It may be a lengthy method to encourage a consumer to download a brand-specific app or search through various platforms of social networking to connect with corporations on a platform with the correct branded account. Under certain cases, consumers could instead churn or engage in derogatory WOM instead of working with the company to raise some concerns.

It looks as if the immediate future of social media customer support is more successful and far-reaching. In a recent review of the future of customer relationship management as to possible mechanisms that allow consumer engagement accessible and functional for consumers, Haenlein (2017) describes Binvisible CRM^.

Managerially speaking, companies are beginning to re-spend as a repercussion of studies highlighting a negative relationship between social media and negative wellbeing. For example, Facebook has created Bedtime limit^ tools (mobile operating systems, such as iOS, now also have these time-

We believe that companies will be able to recreate early indications of customer chatter, behavior, or even physiological data problems in the future (e.g., monitoring the senators in our smartwatches) before customers themselves even realize that they are experiencing a problem. WeWork, the collaborative workplace business, gathers information about how employees travel and behave in a workspace, creating highly customized workspaces based on data patterns.

Taking this type of customer care approach will allow for B seamless service, where businesses would be able to identify and advertise consumer issues when they are still small and scattered. At the same time, only a small number of customers experiences problems. Customer healthcare is a leader in this field, where it has been shown to forecast poor healthcare quality using Twitter and review sites (Greaves et al. 2013), listen to patients to analyze trend terminology (Baktha et al. 2017; Padrez et al. 2016), or even predict disease outbreaks (Baktha et al. 2017; Padrez et al. 2016) (Schmidt 2012).

Companies will invest a lot of R&D efforts in developing very good natural language processing, emotional analysis, and speech synthesis tools to understand better and imitate human interactions (Sheth 2017). For example, Duplex, the new AI assistant from Google, can already call services on its own and reserve reservations for its users seamlessly (Welch 2018). In the future, AI systems will serve as enhancers of human capability, enabling us to achieve more, less time, and better outcomes in the future (Guszcza 2018).

This would reduce the need for call centers and agents for advertisers, decrease pain points in operation, and increase consumer comfort (Kaplan and Haenlein 2019). Some, however, raise the question that a loss of compassion and empathy could result from increased reliance on automation. Force (2018) reveals in a new study that engaging with social media brands decreased the empathy of individuals. Google programmed its AI assistant to respond in a nicer way to inform and inspire people to communicate with computers in a similar way they do with humans, in response to such questions, if you use a friendly approach rather than a com- mandatory approach (Kumparak 2018). While this will help, further study is required to understand the effects on human behavior in an AI-rich environment.

Future research can also analyze how customer-generated data may help businesses predict consumer distress emphatically. The disparity in user interaction between the different channels and the long-term impact of service interactions with non-human AI and IoT will be another important direction for study to better understand.

Social media is a forum for ideas and viewpoints to be expressed. In the case of disseminating political feelings, this is particularly valid. Famously, the win of

President Barack Obama in the 2008 election was due in part to his ability to push.

Involving and engaging voters on social media (Carr, 2008). Indeed, Bond et al. (2012) found that social media sites can increase the probability of voting for specific audiences with simple interventions. Social media, also known as the Arab Spring, is considered one of the main drivers of the 2010 wave of revolutions in the Arab (Brown et al., 2012).

Although social media is not new to politics, we agree that social media is transitioning in the intermediate future to take a far greater role as a political weapon. The first proof of this could be seen in the U.S. presidential election of 2016, when social media took on a new nature, with many perceived temptations to manipulate the views, emotions, and actions of voters. For the then-candidate and Now-President Donald Trump, this is particularly true.

During the campaign, his use of Twitter gained a lot of attention and has continued to do so during his time of office. Yet with a recent example of Congresswoman Alexandria Ocasio-Cortez, who also ran a workshop for fellow congress members on social media, many lawmakers have changed the way they function and communicate with constituents (Dwyer 2019).

Although such platforms enable ideas and concepts to be rapidly disseminated (Bonilla and Rosa 2015; Bode 2016), there are those who have raised ethical concerns about the use of social media for political purposes in both academia and industry. This behavior is said to potentially create echo chambers, where users are only exposed to ideas by like-minded individuals, showing increased political hemophilia, given that people choose who to follow (Bakshy et al., 2015).

The preference of people to team up with like-minded individuals is not new. Social groups have been shown to facilitate social identity and encourage members of the community to adhere to similar ideas (Castano et al., 2002; Harton and Bourgeois 2004). In addition, it has also been shown that group members strongly disassociate and distance themselves from members of the outgroup (Berger and Heath 2008; White and Dahl 2007). Therefore, it is not so shocking to find that personalized social media newsfeeds worsen this issue by creating exclusive news coverage for individual users, trapping them in their supposed echo chambers (Oremus 2016).

Although social media platforms understand that echo chambers can pose a challenge, there is no straightforward solution (Fieger man 2018). One reason why echo chambers pose such a problem is their tendency to consume false news. Fake news is false stories that, in order to manipulate other social media users, attempt to disguise themselves as real content.

In the 2016 U.S. elections, fake news was widely used with claims that foreign governments, such as Iran and Russia, used bots (i.e., automatic online algorithms) to distribute fake information that targeted Hillary Clinton and endorsed President Trump (Kelly et al. 2018). More recently, research has shown how the Chinese government strategically uses thousands of online comments to distract the Chinese public from addressing sensitive issues and promoting nationalism (King et al., 2017). Fake news uses an advanced AI in its current incarnation,

To create ultra-realistic forged photographs and videos of political leaders while manipulating what those leaders mean, a technique called BDeep Fake^ (Schwartz 2018). Such tactics can fool even the sharpest viewer easily. Research has started to explore ways in which social media sites can fight fake news by using algorithms that assess the authenticity of shared content (e.g., Pennycook and Rand 2019). Echo chambers are one aspect that has supported the emergence of fake news.

This happens as the repetitive posting of false news by community members raises awareness and helps (Schwarz and Newman 2017). Bots can only maximize their impact by repeating those posts. Recent research has shown that participants are less likely to fact-check information in a perceived social context, such as social media (Jun et al. 2017), and reject information that does not match well with intuition (Woolley and

Risen 2018). Schwarz and Newman (2017) note that it may be difficult to correct misinformation, especially if the correction is not immediately released, and the false news has already settled into users' minds. It has also been shown that even a single exposure to fake news can have a long-term impact on users, making their impact greater than commonly believed (Pennycook et al., 2019).

Notably, some studies have found that exposure to opposite views (i.e., eliminating online echo chambers) may potentially increase polarisation (versus decrease) (Bail et al., 2018). Therefore, in order to recognize and potentially tackle political extremism, more work from policymakers, corporations, and academics is required. For instance, without censoring free expression, politicians and social media outlets will be actively pressured to fight against Bfake news^. Research that balances the risk of reduced freedom of speech against the harms of spreading false news would also provide theoretical as well as realistic insights.

A Distant Future

In this chapter, we highlight three emerging trends that we believe will affect the future of social media in the long term. Notice that while these patterns are classified as being in the future of Bfar^, many of the problems mentioned here are already present or evolving. They are, however, more complex issues that we believe would take longer to resolve and are of mainstream marketing relevance than the six issues previously addressed in the immediate and near future.

The increased richness of the senses

The bulk of social media posts (e.g., on Facebook, Twitter) were texts in their early days. These platforms soon allowed pictures and then videos to be uploaded, and separate platforms devoted themselves to concentrating on these unique media types (e.g., Instagram and Pinterest for pictures, Instagram for photos, Instagram for images,

And for short images, Snapchat). Such developments have had devasting effects on the use of social media and its implications, as some scientists believe that image-based posts have a greater social impact than text alone (e.g., Pittman and Reich 2016). Importantly, however, a plethora of new technological innovations on the market indicate that social media's future would be more sensory.

One important technology that has already begun to penetrate social media is virtual reality (AR). Snapchat philters, which use the camera of a smartphone to superimpose real-time visual and/or video overlays on people's faces, are perhaps the most recognizable examples of this (including features such as makeup, dog ears, etc.). The company also introduced philters to be directly used on the cats of users (Ritschel 2018). The AR bandwagon was soon followed by other social media players, including Instagram's latest adoption of AR philters (Rao 2017) and Apple's Memoji messaging (Tillman 2018).

This is probably just the example of the iceberg, particularly because Facebook, one of the largest AR technology investors in the industry, has confirmed that it is working on AR glasses (Constine 2018). In particular, the company plans to introduce a developer platform to allow individuals to develop augmented-reality features within Facebook, Instagram, Messenger, and Whatsapp (Wagner 2017). Academic research supports these advances, indicating that AR also offers more authentic (and therefore positive) situated interactions (Hilken et al., 2017). The future of social media is, therefore, likely to look even more visually enhanced, whether viewed through glasses or through conventional smartphone and tablet devices.

Although AR allows users to communicate within their current environments, the user is immersed in other locations through virtual reality (VR), and social media experiences are also increasingly likely to be per- meat by this technology. Although Oculus VR, owned by Facebook, primarily focuses on the fields of immersive gaming and video. At the same time, Facebook Spaces enables friends to connect in virtual reality online and communicate with each other similarly, with the added opportunity to share content (e.g., photos) from their Facebook profiles (Whigham 2018). Avatars are customized to reflect users inside the VR-created space in both cases. When VR technology becomes more affordable and popular (Colville 2018), we believe that social media will eventually play a role in the growing use of technology.

While AR and VR innovations offer visual richness, other advances imply that social media may also be more audible in the future. Hear me out, a new social media player, recently launched a website that allows users to upload and listen to 42-second audio posts (Perry 2018). Enabling users to use social media in a hands-free and eyes-free way not only enables them to connect comfortably with social media.

Multitasking (especially while driving), but the voice is also said to add some wealth and credibility. Since podcasts are more common than ever before (Bhaskar 2018) and voice-based search queries are the fastest-growing form of mobile search (Robbio 2018), it seems likely that this communication modality will show up more in the future as a result of social media use.

Finally, there are early signs that social media in the future will literally feel distinct. Since cell phones are kept in one's hands, and wearable technology is strapped onto one's clothing, businesses and brands are exploring ways to connect through touch with users. Indeed, haptic feedback is increasingly being incorporated into interfaces and applications (technology that recreates the sensation of applying forces, vibrations, or movements to the user; Brave et al. 2001), with aims that go beyond mere alerts of calls or messages. For instance, some businesses are trying to incorporate haptics into advertising content (e.g., users feel their phone shake in mobile advertisements for Stoli vodka as a man shakes a cocktail, mobile games! converts text messages into haptic outputs; Ozcivelek 2015).

Given the high levels of haptic technology expenditure (by 2022, it is projected to be a $20 billion industry; Magnarelli 2018) and the communicative advantages arising from haptic interaction (Haans and IJsselsteijn 2006), we conclude that it is only a matter of time until this approach is incorporated into social media networks.

Future research might examine how the essence of content production and consumption could be altered by some of the new sensory formats described above. Substantively-focused researchers can also explore how these resources may be used by practitioners to develop their services and increase their interactions with clients. It is very important to consider how the distance between online and offline spaces, which is the next theme we are exploring, can be bridged by such sensory-rich formats.

Integration and full integration online/offline

Industry and academics are exploring how advertisers can better combine online and offline efforts (i.e., an omnichannel approach). Industry studies have shown that customers respond better to integrated marketing strategies (e.g., a 73 percent boost over standard email campaigns; Safko 2010). In academia, meanwhile, much of the research considering online promotions and advertisements has traditionally centered on how customers respond to these tactics by online interventions only (e.g., Manchanda et al. 2006), although this has begun to change.

In recent years, further research has explored offline guidance on omnichannel strategies (Lobschat et al., 2017; Kumar et al., 2017).

Several techniques have been used to follow online and offline advertisements and their effects on behavior, such as the use of hashtags to carry conversations online, call-to-actions, using matching strategies on conventional avenues such as television with social media, considering the interest in integrated marketing strategies over the last few years. Although online/offline marketing convergence strategies are currently in place, we believe that the future will go even further in boundaries between offline and online to not only improve the efficacy of marketing campaigns but to fully change the way consumers and businesses communicate with each other and the way social media affects not only online, buy and buy actions.

For brands, there is a range of potential omnichannel marketing patterns that are important. As described earlier, a remarkable technology has started to infiltrate.

The Augmented Reality of Social Media (AR). The future holds many more possibilities in comparison to what already exists (e.g., Snapchat's philters, Pokémon Go). Ikea, for instance, has been working to develop an AR app that enables users to take pictures of a room at home to show exactly, down to the millimeter scale and lighting in the room, what a piece of furniture will look like in the home of a customer (Lovejoy 2017). Another package of AR exams came from the cosmetics company L'Oréal. In 2014, they launched a mobile app named Makeup Genius for the flagship L'Oréal Paris brand that allowed consumers to digitally try makeup on their phones (Stephen and Brooks 2018).

Since then, for their luxury beauty brand Lancôme, they have created AR applications for hair color and nail polish, as well as incorporating AR into mobile e-commerce websites. In the next stage of offline/online convergence, AR-based digital services such as these are likely to be at heart.

AR and related innovations are expected to go beyond and beyond being a tool to help customers make better buying decisions. Conceivably, AR will be integrated into promotions that combine offline and online acts, similar to promotions that already exist to excite customers and build communities. For instance, social media competitions will progress to the stage where users will vote on the best use of AR technology in accordance with the products of a company.

Another way that the future of social media online/offline convergence needs to be addressed is in the form of a digital self. Drawing on the digital era (Belk 2013), the manner in which online acts are perceived by consumers as important

They may be changing to their offline self. Belk (2013) spoke, for instance, about how customers can be re-embodied by avatars they create to reflect themselves online, influence their offline self, and create a variety of selves.

What does this mean about how customers interact with brands and goods while considering digital selves, moreover? Social networking activity is currently one where brands encourage online customer interaction (Chae et al. 2017; Godes and Mayzlin 2009), but the consequences for how the brand's online social media activities and real-life conduct are combined by these types of actions are unclear. Analysis has started to look into the individual level advice on marketing related effects of a consumer's social media actions (Grewal et al. 2019; John et al. 2017; Mochon et al. 2017; Zhang et al. 2017), but much is still unknown.

Furthermore, while recent research has explored how the device used to produce and display content online affects user expectations and behaviors (e.g., Grewal and Stephen 2019), these issues have not been examined in the context of social media to date. Future research should also examine how digital selves (both those kept offline and those that reside only online), social media actions, and how customers meet and use different channels (i.e., device type, app vs. web page, etc.) influence customer behavior, interpersonal relationships, and brand-related measures (e.g., well- being, loyalty, purchase behaviors).

By non-humans, social media

Social networking has not escaped the buzz that surrounds AI. Indeed, over the last decade, social media sites have been populated by social bots (computer algorithms that automatically create content and communicate with social media users; Ferrara et al. 2016) (Lee et al., 2011), and have become increasingly pervasive.

Experts say, for example, that up to 15% of active Twitter accounts are bots (Varol et al., 2017), and that number appears to be on the rise (Romano 2018). Although academics and practitioners are highly concerned with bot identification (Knight 2018), users do not seem to understand when they communicate on social media with bots (as opposed to other human users) in the vast majority of current cases (Stocking and Sumida 2018). While some of these bots are claimed to be benevolent and even helpful (e.g., functioning as aggregators of information), political disruption has also been shown to undermine them.

Discourse, stealing personal information, and spreading misinformation (as mentioned earlier) (Ferrara et al. 2016).

Social bots, of course, are not only an issue for so-called media consumers but also a nagging issue that plagues marketers. Given that businesses also measure social media marketing effectiveness through metrics such as Likes, Shares, and Clicks, the presence of bots poses an increasing challenge to accurate marketing metrics and ROI estimation methods, such as attribution modeling (Bilton 2014). Similarly, if these bots act as followers of Blake, the importance of the audience of influencers can be inflated (Bogost 2018).

As seen in a New York Times Magazine that documents the market used by some influencers to buy such Bfake^ followers to inflate their social media reach, this can also be used nefariously by individuals and companies (Confessore et al. 2018). There have been perverse incentives to play the game by getting non-human Bfake^ bot followers, as it above in relation to influencer marketing, where it has been commonplace for influencers to be charged for posts at rates proportionate to their followers counts. This, however, erodes consumer trust in the ecosystem of social media, which is a growing problem and a near-term problem for many businesses using social media networks for maritime purposes.

There are times, however, where customers realize that they are dealing with bots and do not seem to mind. For example, despite the fact that they are obviously non-human, a number of virtual influencers (created with CGI, as described earlier) seem to be gathering large audiences (Walker 2018). Lil Miquela, one of the most famous of these virtual influencers, has over 1.5 million Instagram followers despite publicly confessing that BI is not a human being... I am a robot^ (Yurieff, 2018). Future research may seek to understand the underlying attraction of these virtual influencers and the possible boundary conditions of their achievement.

Therapy bots are another group of social bots attracting growing attention. These apps (e.g., BWoebot;^ Molteni 2017) strive to encourage users' mental health by proactively checking on them, Blistening^ and interacting with users at any time and suggesting practices to improve the wellbeing of users (de Jesus 2018). For Bcoach^ users, similar bots are used to help them stop maladaptive habits such as smoking (e.g., QuitGenius; Crook 2018). Interestingly, these agents are considered to be less judgmental by being clearly non-human and may, therefore, be easier for users to trust.

Finally, with the Internet of Things movement, the ability for a variety of tangible products and interfaces to connect through social media has been implemented. In what began as a design experiment, for example, BBrad,^ a connected

The Period Immediate Future Futures Subject Presence on-social The advent of influencers Concerns over social media privacy Combating alienation and loneliness Customer service incorporated A Strategic Weapon for Social Media Sensory Richness Increased Integration and Full Integration online/offline. By Non-Humans Social Media

Consumers today live in a world where most facets of their lives will theoretically overlap with social media, and this digitally activated social interactivity influences culture itself.

Prominent actors in social media are using their power to partner with brands. Companies integrate influencers into their marketing mix and create their own virtual influencers.

Social media user trust is on the decline. Consumers worry about their data privacy, and this concern and mistrust are transmitted to brands and businesses from only the platforms.

Conflicting research exists on social media's role in creating user loneliness and isolation, which contributes to calls to revolutionize social media use.

Social networking, the use of enhanced analytics tools, and unparalleled consumer awareness would allow almost Binvisible^ customer service. Customers can connect with companies seamlessly from almost any computer.

Politicians use a social app to communicate directly with voters, evoking various new problems for politicians, such as heightened division, echo chambers, and fake news.

A wealth of emerging technology, including augmented reality, virtual reality, voice activation, and the demand for haptic integration, imply that social media's future will become increasingly sensory.

4.3 Future of social media marketing

The ability to interact with other similar toasters and tweet his Bfeelings^ when ignored or underused was granted to the toaster (Vanhemert 2014). Although this experiment was specifically designed to pose concerns about the future of consumer-product relationships (and product-product relationships^), even in the absence of humans, the prevalence of autonomous tangible de- vices implies a future in which they have a Bvoice^ (Hoffman and Novak 2018).

We assume that bots' existence on social media will be more normalized in the future and more regulated, interested in how bots interact and communicate outside of human interaction with each other. For researchers and practitioners alike, this brings up fascinating future research issues. How will the existence of non-humans alter the essence of content production and social media conversation? And how do businesses better account for the involvement of non-humans in their models of attribution?

Future directions for study and conclusions

As it relates to (and is even inspired by) marketing, this paper has introduced nine concepts related to the future of social media. The themes have consequences for people, companies, organizations, and government and public policymakers. Of course, these themes, which reproduce our own thinking and a combination of views from current studies, market analysts, and mainstream public discourse, are not the full story of what social media's future will entail. However, they are a series of significant problems that we believe would be worth considering in academic study and marketing practice.

We present a review of the proposed research directives in Table 2 to promote future research on these subjects and related topics. These are structured around our nine themes and capture several of the previously mentioned study directions proposed. Social networking is already important as a sub-field in the marketing field, and the potential for future research is focused on recognized needs for new knowledge.

It implies that this sub-field will become much more relevant over time, and responses to perplexing questions. Researchers are encouraged to regard the kinds of research directions in Table 2 as examples of problems that they might further explore. In marketing, we often urge researchers to treat social media as a place where fascinating (and sometimes very new) customer habits occur and can be studied. Social media as a collection of network companies and technologies is fascinating, as we discussed earlier in the paper, but it is how people use social media and the related technologies that are ultimate.

Interest in marketing scholars and experts. Therefore, at the cost of understanding the activities associated with such technologies and networks, we advise scholars not to be excessively enticed by the technological Bshiny new toys^.

Finally, though we relied heavily upon (though not exclusively) on North American examples to explain the emerging trends, by specifically discussing cross-cultural variations in social media use, there are probably important insights to be drawn. Union) can, for example, lead to substantial variations in the manifestation of confidence and privacy concerns. Social media as a political weapon could also be more powerful in regions where the news media is notoriously dominated and censored by the government (e.g., as was the case in many of the Arab Spring countries). Although such cross-cultural variation is beyond this specific paper's reach, we assume that it represents a field of great theoretical and practical importance for future study.

We also concluded that this is a field that is still very much in a state of flux when analyzing the social media environment and contemplating where it is going in the sense of consumer and marketing practice. In marketing, the future of social media is exciting but also unpredictable. We must understand social media better if nothing else, because it has become highly culturally significant, a dominant means of communication and language, a major media type used by advertisement and other types of communication firms, and geopolitical implications. We hope that many fresh ideas and analyses are inspired by the ideas discussed here, which we eventually hope to see being listed and posted through any social media platform.

Acknowledgments The authors thank the editors and reviewers of the special issue for their input and endorse this study by the Oxford Future of Marketing Initiative. The writers contributed equally and are classified from highest to lowest in alphabetical order or, if chosen, Marvel superhero fandom and from lowest to highest in Bon Jovi fandom.

Chapter 5: The Marketing Plan for Social Media

5.1 Introducing

At a phenomenal rate, the world of digital media marketing is evolving. The technologies that are continuously emerging and the way people use them. These make people fill their lifestyle and capture all the knowledge they need by an efficient process. Increasingly advanced technology creation brings new tools and innovations to the fore. Thanks to advanced technology, entrepreneurs benefit from technology, particularly with the presence of numerous social media and marketing strategies.

According to Dr. Ir Eddy Soeryanto Soegoto, marketing is a product that needs to be marketed in the form of products and services that can be recognized, understood, and liked by the public or consumers. The marketing process must be organized through a good marketing strategy to achieve full profits by analyzing the current income situation, including possibilities and setting targets and designing marketing strategies. [3] According to Tito Siswanto, the emergence of more sophisticated technologies and information promotes a transition from traditional communication to modern digital communication. The net is an important element in the development of modern marketing communications to facilitate such communication. Until eventually, it appeared that online social media provided ease of marketing contact with online systems. Owing to the cost and ease of access, it is not unusual for these media companies to sell their goods. [4]

According to Varadarajan, R, marketing strategies can be characterized as an integrated organizational decision-making pattern that defines critical choices for goods, markets, marketing activities, and marketing resources in the manufacture, communication, and/or delivery of products that in exchange with the organization, give value to customers and thus allow the organization to achieve certification. Questions on how company marketing strategies are affected by demand-side variables and supply-side variables are among the fundamental questions for strategic marketing as a field of research.

Attribution to the author(s) and the article's title, journal citation, and DOI of this work must be maintained. Published by IOP Publishing Ltd 1 under license

[5] According to Ozuem, Wilson, the current supply forces companies to respond by adopting customer experience management strategies aimed at customer loyalty. The most profitable thing to build close relationships with consumers is such tactics, which consider all customer experiences. [6] Some service providers will adopt pure transaction marketing tactics, according to Rust, Roland T., Katherine N. Lemon, and Valarie A. Zeithaml. Also, highly standardized service operations require direct customer interaction, and consumers genuinely felt the manufacturing and distribution process.

Therefore, part-time marketers and practical quality effects exist, but we should not speak about pure marketing circumstances for transactions. However, the more common this process is, the more dominant the core resources and technological efficiency of the manufacturing and distribution processes are. The less challenging it is to manage workers from a marketing point of view.

According to Thackeray, Rosemary, where users monitor contact, the second generation of Internet-based applications (i.e., Web 2.0) holds the promise of substantially growing promotional efforts in social media campaigns. By generating and transmitting knowledge through collaborative writing, content sharing, social networking, social bookmarking, and syndication, Web 2.0 applications will directly involve customers in the creative process.

By raising the pace at which customers exchange views and thoughts with a broader audience, Web 2.0 will also increase the power of viral marketing. [8] Sonja Gensler, Peter S.H., according to Lisettede Vries. Leeflanga Social media is an excellent means of promoting customer relations. One specific way to do this is to build a fan page on social networking sites for a company. Brand posts may be placed by firms (containing videos, messages, quizzes, information, and other material).

According to Nina Michaelidou, George Christodoulides Nikoletta Theofania Siamagka, Various resources can support B2B brands, including the internet and other interactive technologies. Nevertheless, research is still limited about how companies use Social Networking Sites (SNS) to achieve brand objectives. [10]According to Richard Hanna, Andrew Rohm, Victoria L. Crittenden, customers are playing increasingly active roles with their respective companies and brands in marketing content production. In essence, to meet customers where they 'work online, businesses and companies search for online social media programs and promotions.

According to Yubo Chen, Scott Fay, Qi Wang, Social Media provides customers with an unprecedented forum for publishing their personal assessments of the purchased goods and promoting word of mouth contact. This paper explores the link between the actions of customer posting and marketing variables such as price and product Value and discusses how these partnerships developed as more widespread acceptance was attracted by the Internet and customer review websites.

In the online sales market, which has a huge potential, social media's position is vital in growing economic growth. This research aims to examine social media marketing communication strategies. This analysis uses a descriptive approach to provide a full picture of the situation linked to several investigation variables. Such findings make social media one of the appropriate media to offer a marketing interaction. It is expected that this marketing strategy can assist online sellers in managing their business.

2. Method Approach

This study used a descriptive approach to find out the variables related to Strategy and Marketing in Social Media and the sources related to the analysis. So it will examine how much social media marketing affects.

3. Results and Debate

Since the era has all been using technology, especially Instagram, the social one most frequently visited by the world community, the thing to do in the marketing strategy here is to sell their goods to attract buyers' attention [12]. Using individuals popular in marketing, with discounts or deals provided good service by uploading items sold with unique photos.

Sample Strategic Strategy on Social Media

The operational goals to achieve the primary social media objectives defined on behalf of [Company Name] by McNelley Media are included in this strategy.

Goals for Social Media Examples

1. Increase the "member" base, employ new members," attract physical traffic to a facility. Purpose: making money/staying in business

2. Brand the name, cause, and facility of [company] as a place of quality treatment, set up [company] as experts

a. Purpose: To manage the image of the company]

3. Keep up to date with the local community on happenings, discounts, holidays, etc.

a. Objective: to increase the number of "members."

4. Understand how social media is used by' members' and track what' members think about

[the company]

a. Purpose: to remain linked with "members."

5. To inform them that [company provides [specific service] a. Contact local community companies. Purpose: word of mouth; to spread the [company] word;

Sample Overview of Online Presence Current

1. To Twitter

a. Known Page

b. Lack of consistent operation, maintenance, leadership

2. Twitter - No attendance

3. Blog - No attendance

4. YouTube - No channel available

5. LinkedIn-No attendance

6. Yelp Yelp

a. Defined Listing

b. Issues with listing, less than 1 hour a week management

c. Conference call set up to reconcile problems with Yelp account manager

Twitter.com/mcnelleymedia facebook.com/mcnelleymedia

Claire Adams McNelley

CEO/Gründer

McNelley Media networks

949,436.9098

Styles of Material

1. Pictures

2. Expert Articles

3. Testimonials on Camera

Tools to Monitor

1. Insights on Facebook

2. Summaries by Hoot Suite Ow.ly

3. Insights on YouTube

Channels of Emphasis

1. Purpose on Facebook:

The Performance Metrics:

2. Purpose on Twitter:

The Performance Metrics:

Objective: Purpose:

The Performance Metrics:

4. LinkedIn Objective:

The Performance Metrics:

5. Purpose for the Blog:

The Performance Metrics:

6. YouTube Programs

Objective: Purpose:

The Performance Metrics:

4. Reminders of Member 5. The Mailers

4. Analytics for Google 5. Analytics from LinkedIn

3. Yelp Yelp

Increase awareness, improve social interaction, create social networks online, search ability

"Like"s, social network referrals

Increase awareness, increase engagement, network establishment, brand establishment, search ability

Followers, 2nd-order followers (followers count), social capital (Twitter followers influence), Klout ranking, referrals

"Management of credibility, increasing interaction with "members," search ability

Reviews, stars, involvement, referrals

Increase awareness, increase interaction, network establishment, brand establishment, search ability.

5.2 Digitalization in Business" National Level Seminar

Chung and Austria (2010) explored the aims of figuring out whether social media, the attitudes towards social media marketing messages, and the efficacy of online shopping value messages are underlying gratification. The Uses and Gratification Theory (Katz, Bluner & Gurevitch, 1974 and as enhanced by Ruggiero, 2000) was the basis for examining user gratification in social media use. In connection with social media marketing messages, online shopping value was examined.

Entertainment, results, and interaction were taken as exogenous variables for social media gratification. The endogenous variables were the attitude towards social media marketing messages and online shopping concepts. This critical study on sustainable marketing and social media, involving cross-culture populations (subjects) to examine sustainable behaviors' motivations, was done by Minton, Lee, Orth, Kim, and Kahle (2012). South Koreans represent the collectivist culture, and the United States was studied based on their use of Facebook and Twitter on motives for sustainable behaviors.

Germany is more of an individualistic culture. Using Kelman's (1958) practical motivations as a fundamental theoretical basis, the online survey approach was used to cover subjects belonging to various cultures. This study's conceptual model attempted to investigate how sustainable practices such as recycling behaviors, organic food buying, green transport usage, anti-materialistic attitudes, and charity are influenced by functional motivations (responsibility, engagement, and internalization).

This exploratory study, based on primary data, was conducted by Vinerean, Cetina, Dumitrescu, and Tichindelean (2013) using university students in Romania to explore how to engage with different types of audiences on social media marketing channels (based on their online behavioral aspects) to optimize the impact of the online marketing strategy. To find out if various predictors linked to web users and social networking sites positively influence consumer perceptions of online ads, a linear model has been tested.

The Marketing Channel Websites of social networking

Websites for social networking allow individuals, companies, and other organizations to connect and create online relationships and communities. When businesses enter these social networks, customers may directly connect with them. That contact can be more intimate for users than conventional outbound marketing and advertisement strategies. Social networking sites serve as word of mouth or e-word of mouth, more specifically.

The Research Goal

Studying Social Media Marketing Digital Marketing Research

To research Patterns in Digital Marketing

Methodologies

Form of Research: Descriptive Type

"Digitalization in Business" National Level Seminar

Websites for social networking are focused on developing virtual communities that allow customers to communicate their wishes, desires, and values online. Marketing on social media then links these customers and viewers to companies who have the same desires, wishes, and values. Companies may keep in contact with individual followers through social networking sites. This personal contact will instill in followers and potential customers a feeling of loyalty.

Often, goods can hit a tiny target audience by selecting whom to follow on these pages—social networking sites give a lot of information on what future buyers may be involved in goods and services. Marketers can identify purchase signs, such as content exchanged by individuals and questions posed online, using emerging semantic analysis technologies. An awareness of purchasing signs will help salespeople target specific customers, and marketers manage micro-targeted campaigns.

Over 80% of company executives listed social media as an important part of their company in 2014. Company retailers have seen a rise of 133 percent in their social media marketing sales.

Mobile handsets

In the world, over three billion people are involved on the Internet. The Internet has steadily attracted more and more users over the years, jumping from 738 million in 2000 all the way to 3.2 billion in 2015. In the United States, about 81 percent of the existing population has a social media profile that they regularly communicate with.

For social media marketing, cell phone use is useful because mobile phones have social networking features, allowing users to search the web quickly and access social networking sites. Mobile phones have evolved exponentially, radically altering the path-to-purchase process by enabling customers to quickly access real-time pricing and product details and enable businesses to remind and update their followers continuously.

Many businesses now placed QR (Quick Response) codes and items to access their smartphones on the company website or online services. By linking the code to brand websites, ads, product details, or any other mobile-enabled content, retailers use QR codes to promote customer engagement with brands. Real-time bidding in the mobile advertising industry is also strong and growing because of its appeal for web surfing on-the-go. A 37% rise in revenue per month was announced in 2012 by Nexage, a real-time bidding provider in mobile ads. A rise of 22 billion ad requests that same year was announced by Adfonic, another mobile advertisement publishing site.

Mobile devices have become increasingly popular, with 5.7 billion people worldwide using them. This has played a role in how media communicate with viewers and has many more ramifications for TV ratings, ads, mobile commerce, and more. The consumption of mobile media, such as mobile audio streaming or mobile video, is growing

. More than 100 million users are expected to access online video content through mobile devices in the United States. Mobile video income consists of downloads, advertisements, and subscriptions for pay per view. As of 2013, internet user penetration of cell phones worldwide was 73.4 percent. E more than 90 percent of Internet users will access online content from their phones in 2017, estimates say.

Digital Marketing Effect of Social Media Marketing Trends

In every SEO digital marketing campaign, the growth of social media marketing channels has become a major part of creating social signals that are very important. You may not realize that the advent of multiple social media platforms presents a broader marketing opportunity for internet marketers like you to create brand awareness across the web. How your website ranks on the search engine will have a huge effect on your client, and the acquisition and conversion of leads.

To create the organic website traffic, social media marketing integrated with search engine optimization strategies is successful. The way digital marketers conduct their search engine optimization strategy to improve their lead generation process and website conversion rates would impact various social media marketing trends.

Here are all the social media marketing patterns, from digital marketing experts' perspectives, that can affect your digital marketing and search engine optimization campaigns' growth and effectiveness. Are you able to accept these developments in their internet marketing systems to incorporate them?

Investing in content for social media - A necessity rather than a desire

Online marketers now see from a different angle the importance of social media marketing for their companies. The number of customers who use social services to find the goods and services they need is experiencing a huge explosion. According to prestigious statistics on social consumers:

Around 76 percent of organizations use social networking to accomplish their marketing goals. After marketing their company, business retailers experience an increase in revenue of about 133 percent.

The mobile industry, which promotes the importance of social media marketing for its sector.

40% of US online shoppers use Mobile for in-store shopping.

Approximately 71 percent of consumers react based on feedback and suggestions from

Concerning a specific brand, social users.

Consumer reviews are considered trustworthy by shoppers than marketing promotion reviews.

They come directly from the site of the brand.

Many popular brands have a social media page to broaden their coverage in marketing.

To make their brand more available among users of social media.

Among the advantages of using social media networks in the promotion of a brand are

1. **Social signals that are growing**

Social signals will improve your search engine optimization efforts significantly. The more entities, the more

The more the search can find your website important in the social media community sharing, all search engines find your website relevant. The more your web pages are likely to achieve a higher ranking on the search engine results list.

2. **Promote branding and visibility for companies**

Users of social media can still suggest substantial brand quality to their social media circles. This can be a successful marketing boost to your brand name and become a follower of your brand by raising the number of individuals involved in your brand's credibility. 3. Efficient word of mouth advertisement is

Word of mouth advertising appears to have a higher customer confidence rating than the details of the product that your business promotes from your website. Whenever the social media community receives more views and shares from your web page, your audience's broader reach and impact become for your target clients.

Tariff for your site. To create the organic website traffic, social media marketing integrated with search engine optimization strategies is successful. The way digital marketers conduct their search engine optimization strategy to improve their lead generation process and website conversion rates would impact various social media marketing trends.

Patterns from digital marketing experts' perspectives can affect your digital marketing and search engine optimization campaigns' growth and effectiveness. Are you able to accept these developments in their internet marketing systems to incorporate them?

Investing in content for social media - A necessity rather than a desire Online marketers now see from a different angle the importance of social media marketing for their companies. The number of customers who use social services to find the goods and services they need is experiencing a huge explosion. According to prestigious statistics on social consumers:

Around 76 percent of organizations use social networking to accomplish their marketing goals. After marketing their company, business retailers experience an increase in revenue of about 133 percent.

The mobile industry, which promotes the importance of social media marketing for its sector.

40% of US online shoppers use Mobile for in-store shopping.

Approximately 71 percent of consumers react based on feedback and suggestions from

Concerning a specific brand, social users.

Consumer reviews are considered trustworthy by shoppers than marketing promotion reviews.

They come directly from the site of the brand.

Many popular brands have a social media page to broaden their coverage in marketing.

To make their brand more available among users of social media.

Among the advantages of using social media networks in the promotion of a brand are

1. **Social signals that are growing**

Social signals will improve your search engine optimization efforts significantly. The more entities, the more

All the search engine finds your website important in the social media community sharing, the more the search engine finds your website relevant. The more your web pages are likely to achieve a higher ranking on the search engine results list.

2. **Promote branding and visibility for companies**

Users of social media can still suggest substantial brand quality to their social media circles. This can be a successful marketing boost to your brand name and become a follower of your brand by raising the number of individuals involved in your brand's credibility. 3. Efficient word of mouth advertisement is

Word of mouth advertising appears to have a higher customer confidence rating than the details of the product that your business promotes from your website. Whenever the social media community receives more views and shares from your web page, your audience's broader reach and impact become for your target clients.

It is also important for achieving your marketing objectives to incorporate social media into your digital marketing strategy. With the need to incorporate it into digital marketing to make small to medium businesses at par and competitive with their rivals, social media marketing becomes a significant pillar in SEO from being a mere luxury means of marketing business online.

"Digitalization in Business" National Level Seminar

In digital marketing, the social advertising trend is becoming important.

Because of the trend in customers' purchasing habits, digital marketers are drawn to social media ads. Social media surveys show that a significant percentage of customers spend on popular social media platforms such as Facebook and Twitter an average of 37 minutes a day, and 10 percent of internet users spend on social media sites. Imagine the future consumer advantage for online marketers that social media can offer. Around 53 percent of digital marketers have already placed their brand in the social media sector in 2013, and social ads' investment will continue to rise by 2014. If your company does not take this marketing measure by now to expand your business reach, your rivals are likely to take advanced measures with a stronger and bigger market opportunity to play around.

It is important to incorporate the following to exploit social advertising to your business advantage: Identifying measurable objectives for your business.

Integrate social ads into your optimization plan for search engines to optimize your Efforts and effects in marketing.

Identify the actions, desires, and behaviors of your target client by using SEO analytics.

The future efficacy of the social advertising strategy will be evaluated.

Used while the target group is engaged.

Optimizing the website's landing pages by incorporating SEO and social media marketing

Tactics. Don't underestimate social media buttons' power.

Image-Centric material for ads on social media

Users of social media are becoming more interested in posting and liking photos Picture content can be very appealing to social media users that give a good brand's online visibility. The image-centered content has become one of Atlanta's social media marketing companies' social media marketing patterns incorporated into their search engine optimization strategies under the theory that mages are considered to increase the visibility of a brand to search engine users.

Social incorporation into the marketing of emails

Digital marketers regard email marketing as one of the foundations of successful lead conversion. Despite the recent trend in digital marketing, the widespread use of email marketing continues to be prevalent, and marketers are taking the initiative of leveraging social media marketing to improve their business lead conversions further. Your leaders would find it easier to make a purchasing decision by using social media if they see your brand in their peers' social feeds. In their social media status updates, social media marketers typically use updating their email marketing content, which effectively promotes brand marketing updates.

The research began with the goal of analyzing the various issues associated with digital marketing. Based on the discussion, it was found that the most important aspect in the case of digital marketing is to communicate with users. The commitment ladder showed approaches to consumer attachment. The study also revealed that businesses are expected to design an effective platform to use digital marketing effectively. The efficacy of a social media site was explored with the example of Interest. In the report, the latest developments in digital marketing were also addressed. It has shown that integrating all the structures with that of the digital network has become important in the current context. The emerging digitalization developments have been exemplified by the transition of a newspaper from a printed edition to an online version.

Conclusion

There are some of the significant mistakes made by businesses that lead them to miss out on the benefits of social media, especially in the sense of marketing. The researcher personally assumes that it is important for organizations to first build an efficient communication campaign to take full advantage of social media for marketing and promotion. The methodology should be in accordance with the goals and objectives of the company. The researcher further analyses that it is also important for the organization to actively maintain and monitor all of its social media pages, blogs, and accounts and respond promptly to the queries and comments of people